Discerning Beyond
the Screen

Discerning Beyond the Screen

Embracing Christian-Based Films as a Spiritual Discipline for Spiritual Formation and Discipleship

Toya D. Booth

RESOURCE *Publications* · Eugene, Oregon

DISCERNING BEYOND THE SCREEN
Embracing Christian-Based Films as a Spiritual Discipline for Spiritual Formation and Discipleship

Copyright © 2024 Toya D. Booth. All rights reserved. Except for brief quotations in critical publications or reviews, no part of this book may be reproduced in any manner without prior written permission from the publisher. Write: Permissions, Wipf and Stock Publishers, 199 W. 8th Ave., Suite 3, Eugene, OR 97401.

Resource Publications
An Imprint of Wipf and Stock Publishers
199 W. 8th Ave., Suite 3
Eugene, OR 97401

www.wipfandstock.com

PAPERBACK ISBN: 979-8-3852-2157-8
HARDCOVER ISBN: 979-8-3852-2158-5
EBOOK ISBN: 979-8-3852-2159-2
VERSION NUMBER 07/22/24

Scripture quotations are taken from the New Revised Standard Version Updated Edition. Copyright © 2021 National Council of Churches of Christ in the United States of America. Used by permission. All rights reserved worldwide.

Scripture quotations marked (NIV) are taken from the Holy Bible, New International Version®, NIV®. Copyright © 1973, 1978, 1984, 2011 by Biblica, Inc.™ Used by permission of Zondervan. All rights reserved worldwide. www.zondervan.com The "NIV" and "New International Version" are trademarks registered in the United States Patent and Trademark Office by Biblica, Inc.™

Scripture quotations marked (NLT) are taken from the Holy Bible, New Living Translation, copyright ©1996, 2004, 2015 by Tyndale House Foundation. Used by permission of Tyndale House Publishers, Carol Stream, Illinois 60188. All rights reserved.

To My First Love, Jesus Christ.
In whom I have come to know more deeply,
embrace fully, and offer my greatest love.

"God, make me so uncomfortable that I will do the very thing I fear."
—Ruby Dee

Contents

List of Diagrams | ix
Preface | xi
Acknowledgments | xv

Introduction | 1
1　Spiritual Formation | 11
2　Storytelling, Parables, and Christian-based Films' Significance in Spiritual Formation | 25
3　Establishment and Flourishing of Cinema's Influence and Responses | 45
4　Embracing Christian-based Films as a Prospective Spiritual Discipline | 74
Conclusion: Encountering The Miracle of Spiritual Formation Through Christian-based Films | 108

Appendix | 117
Bibliography | 131

List of Diagrams

Diagram 1: Framework for Viewing Christian-based Films as a Spiritual Discipline | 78

Preface

In the tapestry of my life, ministry threads have woven through every chapter, shaping my identity and purpose in profound ways. From the early days as a youth leader, navigating the harmonies of bi-vocational leadership, to ministering through the unexpected twists of adulthood, I have emerged as a pastoral leader, educator, creative, and entrepreneur. These roles have enriched my path with diverse experiences and even greater challenges. With exposure to people, places, politics, and predicaments both inside the church and within secular spaces, each step demanded a deeper reliance on my faith in Christ. My journey has been a testament to the transformative power of seeking to have a deeper personal relationship with Jesus Christ. Moreover, these experiences have provided insight into the dilemma the church faces in making disciples and ensuring their spiritual maturity, thereby keeping them strong in the faith.

Amidst the evolving landscape of ministry leadership, which has led me through diverse spheres—from pulpits to conference stages and classrooms to boardrooms—one constant has remained: the call to illuminate hope and possibility, even in the darkest of times. I recall a poignant moment from my childhood involving a story my grandfather used to tell me. At just around five years old, I unknowingly became a vessel for the Holy Spirit's reassurance to my grandfather during a work crisis he was facing as a leader at a community gathering. In a time of uncertainty, I was used to discern and assure him that everything would be alright. That early encounter, etched in memory, became a foundational stone in my ministry path, reaffirming my purpose to inspire faith and resilience in others.

The church has been the foundation of my spiritual formation and affirmation. Through my relationships within the church, I have developed

Preface

the discipleship tools necessary for ministry leadership. Often, spiritual transformation comes in what we consider the simple moments in life, requiring us to discern that God is often moving in the things we overlook or consider insignificant, like the voice of a child whispering in our ear that everything is going to be alright.

However, we must first see the challenges before us, admit there is a problem to address, acknowledge our contribution to the conundrum, and surrender to the recognition that God has the answers. Throughout my journey, from youth leadership to my vocation as a ministry leader, I have witnessed the church's declining influence. Our issues are not just in the decline of church attendance but also in our impact on culture.

Like many church and ministry leaders, I have found myself in a place of uncertainty, unsure of how to minister to a generation that no longer sees the church as relevant and questions if Jesus is real or if He truly is the answer. Pastoral and ministry leaders grapple with understanding the way forward, seeking the Lord to reveal the methods to navigate this challenge. Consequently, numerous studies, theories, initiatives, collaborations, discussions, and recommendations circulate in hopes of finding ways to reach the people and generations for whom the Gospel has been lost in cultural and generational translation.

Yet, as the tides of culture shift and the influence of the church wanes, the urgency to rediscover our relevance and resonance in society becomes ever more palpable. In this tumultuous landscape, I feel compelled to offer a beacon of hope to fellow ministry leaders, educators, and laypersons, beckoning them to rise above the disheartening statistics and embrace innovative approaches. Our goal is to grow in a deeper relationship with Jesus Christ and to teach others to do likewise through discipleship.

Thus, this book emerges as a testament to the transformative potential of an unconventional yet profoundly impactful tool: Christian-based films. Through personal reflection and ministry experiences, I've unearthed a rich vein of spiritual formation and discipleship within the captivating narratives of cinema.

Sharing my research, insights, and passion for spiritual formation and film is fueled by the burden I feel to look every Christian leader and believer in the eyes and say, "Everything is going to be alright." As followers of Christ, especially as church leaders, we must not become consumed by disturbing statistics and the challenges of our declining influence. Instead, we must consider how we arrived at this place, assess which aspects of our

Preface

ministry is fruitful or no longer viable, and rethink how we minister with intentionality as the Holy Spirit reveals how to fulfill the Great Commission in popular culture.

The work I offer for consideration is rooted in my love for Jesus Christ, my gratitude for the positive influence of the church in my life, and my passion for providing solutions for equipping the Body of Christ in Christian spiritual formation. I aim to help the church navigate the challenges we face in discipleship. Furthermore, it is imperative that we confront how our own spiritual perspectives may be hindered by traditions, doctrine, theology, and dogma, which can impede our spiritual growth in Christ and our efforts in discipleship.

I present a pathway that has been revealed to me through personal and ministry experiences engaged in watching movies. The stories that have been dramatically displayed on screens present the Gospel of Jesus Christ and the impact of living a life in Christ in a way that has led to me experiencing and witnessing spiritual transcendence and transformation for myself and others. My prayer is that as you engage the information, I present to you in the forthcoming pages, you will surrender to the Holy Spirit what you have come to know and understand about spiritual formation and discipleship, to consider what the Lord wants to reveal to you with transformative results.

Since completing research for my central argument claim, at least six Christian-based or Faith-based films have been released in movie theaters over the past year, with at least another five slated for release throughout 2024. Three of the recently released films have particularly convinced me that God is using movies to spiritually reach people, addressing areas where the church has faced challenges in sharing the message of Jesus Christ.

What stands out about these three films is that they are all biopics, based on true stories. I am clear that while these films offer creative interpretations of what the church understands as testimonies, they also represent how Jesus Christ is actively moving among us. As Scripture says, "But they have conquered him by the blood of the Lamb and by the word of their testimony."[1] I am convinced that we, as followers of Christ, will overcome all that we face by continuing to share our testimonies and embracing those of others.

In conclusion, consider embracing the testimony shared through *Ordinary Angels* (2024), based on the true story of the Schmitt family from

---

1. Rev 12:11 (NRSVUE).

my hometown of Louisville, KY. Their testimony resonates deeply with its portrayal of faith amidst adversity. Having had the privilege of interviewing Ashley Schmitt on my podcast, "Phoenix Faith", I was deeply moved by her family's journey through challenges and miracles, as portrayed on the silver screen.

Open your heart to embrace films like *Cabrini* (2024). This story offers a compelling glimpse into the life of Francesca Cabrini, a Catholic missionary whose unwavering faith transformed the lives of impoverished communities in late nineteenth-century New York City. Witnessing her tireless dedication to God's call, despite insurmountable odds, instilled in me a renewed sense of faith and determination to serve, regardless of the personal challenges I face.

Lastly, hear the message of possibilities communicated through *Unsung Hero* (2024). The film chronicles the remarkable journey of the Smallbone family, renowned figures in Christian Contemporary music. Their story of faith, perseverance, and humility serves as a poignant reminder of God's faithfulness amidst life's trials and tribulations.

As we journey together through the pages ahead, let us delve deeper into the profound themes and spiritual truths embedded within all of the cinematic masterpieces presented as viable spiritual disciplines. They bring the Gospel of Jesus Christ to the ends of the world and offer us the opportunity to experience transcendence. May the stories we encounter ignite flames of inspiration and revelation, guiding us ever closer to the heart of God through Jesus Christ.

Acknowledgments

Foremost, without God, none of what I have accomplished on my journey would be possible, and I am eternally grateful. I remain prayerful that all I do will bring glory to Elohim and my Savior, Jesus Christ.

I am grateful to all my relatives, friends, colleagues, and family of believers who have faithfully and lovingly journeyed with me and continue to do so. Your circle of support has been the wind beneath my wings, the arms that have held me up, the prayers that have constantly covered me, and the laughter that has lifted my spirits and helped me carry on. I express my heartfelt gratitude to all who have supported me in life, ministry, and education, at whatever point the Lord allowed our paths to cross, no matter how brief or long.

A special thank you to my Duke Divinity School dissertation supervisor, Dr. Dan Train, and my spiritual formation consultant, Rev. Sonia Crawley, who have enthusiastically guided me during my research, study, and writing. Your invaluable insight, wisdom, knowledge, and tireless support in helping me forge a path less traveled and advocating for this work to be published is greatly appreciated. Thank you to Dr. Will Willimon, Director of the Doctor of Ministry Program at Duke Divinity, for helping to ensure my finished work has the opportunity to reach the masses.

Introduction

On Saturday, August 24th, 2019, at 1 PM EST, I went to the movie theater to see the Christian film, *Overcomer* (2019).[1] The Kendrick Brothers created the film and are also credited with the movies *Facing the Giants* (2006), *Fireproof* (2008), *Courageous* (2011), and *War Room* (2015).[2] I had viewed their previous work and greatly anticipated this new release from followers of Christ who have contributed to the Christian film industry as faith leaders. As an instructor and minister of spiritual formation, I have incorporated the Kendrick Brothers' films into my curricula, studies, and ministry activities. Despite my familiarity with their work, I had a transcendent and transformative encounter the day I saw *Overcomer*. While viewing the movie, a spiritual rousing within me began percolating as a connection was made between the characters and me as I was dealing with similar emotional and spiritual dilemmas at the time. The specific scenarios were drastically different. However, the vantage points that needed clarity were similar and tugged at my heart while pulling me along spiritually, mentally, emotionally, and physically to the very conclusion of the film.

I felt a transcendent connection I had not experienced before in a movie theater. Much about the experience was familiar; everything I was taking in was overwhelming, comforting, and transforming at various stages of the film and sometimes simultaneously. However, when the song "Overcomer" began to play, and 1 John 5:5—"Who is it that overcomes the world? Only the one who believes that Jesus is the Son of God"—was displayed on the screen as the credits started to roll, I felt as though Jesus was holding me in His arms, and I could conquer anything waiting for

1. Kendrick, *Overcomer*.
2. Kendrick, *Facing the Giants*, *Fireproof*, and *Courageous*.

me outside that theater.[3] I was having an encounter with the Holy Spirit that was just like the encounters that I experienced countless times in the sanctuary of the churches where I worshiped, the pulpits I have ministered from, and during sacred moments in which I have engaged the presence of the Triune God. In the theater on that August day, I recognized what I have defined as a "God Moment," a moment in time when the Spirit of God meets me where I am in my life, touches my heart in the most intimate parts, speaks to my spirit in a way that is precise and clear, and moves me to a place of transformation that leaves me forever changed.

During my time at the theater, I worshiped in song, received the revelation of Scripture, sought God in prayer, and praised God for the message spoken to me through the art of film. After seeing *Overcomer*, I left the movie theater, and no one could convince me that I had not just left the church. I felt like I had been to the house of the Lord and worshiped God in spirit and in truth.[4] In fact, my encounter was so powerful that I purchased a ticket for the next day and went to see the movie again as an intentional spiritual act of worship. I went even further by looking up Scriptures that the movie emphasized and sought the Lord for greater understanding during times of meditation. I recognized that the film served as a spiritual discipline that led to my spiritual growth and took me through a process that deepened my relationship with Jesus Christ.

Since then, in my spiritual discipline practice of meditation and reflection, I realized that movies have always been a means that God has used to lead me to clarity and build interpersonal connections in my life. Growing up, watching movies was more than entertainment; it was an opportunity to travel to the unexpected alone or take a journey with my loved ones and friends. My earliest memories are of the connection my father and I had of watching movies and later having him unexpectedly engage me in a trivia pursuit of recalling famous movie lines and pairing a soundtrack or characters to a film. My father and I built an intimacy around films that only we understood and appreciated. This shared passion brought joy to our hearts and cultivated a bond that has persisted throughout my adulthood.

As I look back over my life and consider how the Triune God has communicated with me and through me, films have a consistent fingerprint along my spiritual journey and formation. Much like the bond my father and I formed over movie trivia, The Lord has used the visual arts

---

3. Mandisa, "Overcomer" and 1 John 5:5 (NIV).
4. John 4:24.

Introduction

medium to connect, guide, teach, chastise, bring joy, and lead me beside still waters.[5] For me, watching movies has been a sacred, safe, and happy place to explore places, emotions, and thoughts that reality often hindered experiencing. Whether in a theater, community venue, or the privacy of my home, watching films has been a spiritual and emotional connection that has influenced how I understand and communicate the things I often cannot put into words. Even more profoundly, I began to recognize how the Holy Spirit spoke to me through several movies, supporting my spiritual growth journey and making me feel closer to Jesus Christ.

As movies bonded my father and me while increasing our cinema knowledge, the Triune God did something much deeper within me. I developed discernment to look beyond the screen and intimately connect with spiritual understanding. There was an emotional connection and spiritual language between the Triune God and me that only we understood. The Holy Spirit moved within and around me that August summer day to make sense of what I was experiencing during that time in my life, instructed me on how to continue my faith journey, and encouraged me to keep pressing forward. Those messages came through the silver screen for me in a movie theater. As I opened myself up to the Spirit of God and discerned beyond the screen, I was spiritually formed and transformed in an unexpected way.

ATTESTING TO THE TRANSFORMATIVE POWER OF FILM

Looking beyond my own cinema encounters, I have discovered other theologians, pastoral leaders, and disciples of Christ who have also had transcendent and transformative experiences while viewing films. I have also witnessed how films have impacted other people I have engaged personally, academically, and in ministry. All of these entities, and the ones I will continue to share, have been a guiding force for the central argument claim I am presenting.

For example, Dr. James Merritt is a pastor, author, and national voice on faith and leadership. In his book, *52 Weeks with Jesus: Fall in Love with the One Who Changed Everything*, he accounts how an experience at a movie theater helped him fall in love with Jesus.[6] Merritt tells readers about his conversion experience when his mother took him and his brother to the movie theater one Friday after school as a child. He did not know what the

---

5. Ps 23:2.
6. Merritt, *52 Weeks with Jesus*, 13–16.

movie would be about, but he was excited about the experience he rarely had as a nine-year-old. When the movie started, he was surprised that Jesus appeared on the screen. Merritt explains that he had heard stories about Jesus his entire life and knew that Jesus loved him through those stories, but he had never seen Jesus in the stories.[7] Although Merritt had heard of the story of Jesus being crucified, it was not until he saw the crucifixion of Jesus come to life on screen before him that he was spiritually moved to respond. He described the moment as follows:

> A response pierced the darkness and penetrated my heart: "They are not crucifying him. You are!" Breath was sucked out of my lungs and my stomach turned. What was I to make of such an accusation? I rode to my own defense. Me? I wasn't there when they crucified Jesus.
>
> The scene progressed, and I assumed the conversation had ended. I declared myself winner by TKO. But then the voice returned again: "Remember, he died for your sins." The voice was right. The Roman soldiers and spikes weren't the only ones that nailed Jesus to the cross. My sins affixed him there. In some way, I had scourged him, brutalized him, defaced him, humiliated him, spat on him, mocked him, and condemned him. He died for me, because of me, and instead of me.
>
> And that is the moment I realized it:
>
> There's nobody like Jesus.
>
> I prayed: Jesus, I believe you died for my sins. I believe you came back from the dead. There is no one else like you. Please forgive me and save me. Amen.
>
> I sat still for a moment, not sure if I had done anything at all. I didn't feel different. A choir of angels didn't serenade me, no bright lights shone down on my seat, and a deep bass voice didn't shout, "I am God. Welcome into my family." Still, I knew that the boy who was going to walk out of the Royal Theater was not the one who had walked in. I elbowed my mom, and before she could shush me, I whispered, "Momma, I think I just got saved. I just asked Jesus into my heart."[8]

Clearly, Merritt had a transcendent and transformative experience while watching a movie. He encountered the Holy Spirit in the movie theater, who engaged his imagination through the film to bring salvation into his life. Merritt was a child free from bias, judgment, and criticism. He was

---

7. Merritt, *52 Weeks with Jesus*, 14.
8. Merritt, *52 Weeks with Jesus*, 14–15.

Introduction

unknowingly spiritually open, going to have an enjoyable experience with his family at the movies that ended up changing his life. Merritt's spiritual encounter was the start of his love journey with Jesus Christ and the Holy Spirit's method to begin his spiritual growth and deepen his relationship with Jesus Christ. The film started a journey of spiritual formation as Merritt responded to the message he received that day in the movie theater.

Merritt's testimony raises the question: How should a pastor or faith leader respond when they hear of someone having an experience like Merritt's? How do we intentionally come alongside someone and nurture their spiritual growth through the means God used to engage them? We must acknowledge the transformational power of the stories that come to life on movie screens. Developing our ability to discern how Christian-based films are capable of acting as a spiritual discipline and creating opportunities to nurture believers and seekers to connect spiritually with Christ can be life-changing. The spiritual transformation potential through the medium of Christian-based films can be a personal experience, as well as a corporate encounter that churches can explore as a way of discipleship.

As a seminary adjunct professor and minister of spiritual formation, I have also witnessed films' influence on the spiritual formation of those I have taught. As the Fall courses began in 2011, I decided to take my class on a field trip to the movie theater. The students and I met at a Manhattan movie theater and watched the Kendrick Brothers' new film, *Courageous*, together as an act of spiritual formation. The students were asked to reflect on the themes presented in the movie.[9] Their assignment for the next class was to be prepared to discuss the film in the context of spiritual formation. Students were to consider how the film contributed to their spiritual formation and the potential to be a means of discipleship in their ministries. The class time we spent in the theater was more than an academic assignment; it was also a spiritual discipline exercise. We prayed for insight, studied the film, meditated on the messages, and sought guidance collectively through class discussions. Utilizing film in my higher education curriculum not only provided an alternative way to explore the course material but also contributed to the spiritual development of my students. Watching a film allowed students to navigate between a cognitive, emotional, spiritual, and psychological space to form a perspective that may not have been reached by using a textbook, lectures, and class discussions alone.

9. Kendrick, *Courageous*.

Discerning Beyond the Screen

On another occasion in March 2014, the movie *God's Not Dead* was released in movie theaters.[10] I saw the presentation of the film as an opportunity to invite my church, family, friends, and neighbors to gather at the theater. The ministry's intention was for us to watch together and discuss the faith themes outlined in the movie over a meal at a neighboring restaurant afterward. On the day of our gathering, I had approximately fifteen people show up for the movie theater in Louisville, KY. We met at a reserved space in a local restaurant to break bread, fellowship, and discuss the movie.

Two things stood out to me about the *God's Not Dead* discussion: 1) some people who struggled to attend church joined us for the movie and dinner, and 2) everyone who participated in the discussion was relaxed and willing to share their thoughts openly about the themes presented in the film without feeling judged. We had created a safe spiritual space together. I decided to organize another gathering to watch the film *Heaven is for Real* about a month later, in April 2014.[11] Those in attendance increased slightly because some had invited others to attend. The additional people shifted the group dynamics slightly for our discussion afterward, as I noticed that we had more children present brought by their parents. Parents wanted their children to see a story about a little boy who had a miraculous encounter with Jesus. Again, as we ate a meal and enjoyed being together in the community, I witnessed the power of the Holy Spirit moving among us as we discussed the details of the film.

In facilitating the movie viewing and discussions, I never experienced a complaint about how much the film cost. There were no questions about why we were gathering to watch a film or hesitation to discuss the movie afterward over a meal. I was enlightened to an alternative way to access the people around me and engage them in a spiritually forming activity. The movie fellowship left them unguarded and open to exploring a relationship with Jesus Christ and communing with the people of God outside the church walls. Even for me, I had an encounter with God in a movie theater that far exceeded my expectations as I opened my heart to receive what the Holy Spirit shared with me in viewing *Overcomer*. As I discerned beyond the screen, I realized how deeply I was spiritually formed, brought on by an act of spiritual discipline by watching a Christian-based film.

---

10. Cronk, *God's Not Dead*.
11. Wallace, *Heaven Is for Real*.

Introduction

FILM AS A RESOURCE FOR SPIRITUAL FORMATION

Gareth Higgins is a social justice activist, author, and film enthusiast who offers insight to those seeking to find spirituality in cinema.[12] He makes an appropriate observation concerning Jesus' declaration that those who believe in him would do greater things than he did and was doing.[13]

> There was a time when people would have thought that moving celluloid pictures, animated by light, telling stories was impossible. We would do well to remember this, and in our remembering, be grateful for what cinema can offer. Cinema, often is a miracle itself. Jesus once spoke of the "greater things" that His followers would do, which seems strange for a man who had just raised the dead. But people say He said it, so I guess He meant it. What are the "greater things"? Perhaps mercy, justice, freedom, sight to the blind give us some indication, but I suspect words don't do justice to justice. Being fully human is not the same thing as being part of a particular faith tradition, Christian or otherwise. If we think faith is just a matter of believing the "right" things and trying to persuade others to do the same, we've put the cart before the horse. Surely we must realize that we're all such lonely people, and the struggles facing humanity are so inconceivably great, that belief alone is not going to resolve our condition. To follow Jesus means to invest the time to create space for God to make you human again. We should make time for this.[14]

Like Higgins, this core idea claim argues that films can undoubtedly be miraculous works that God has gifted to humanity. As Christians seeking to be the Body of Christ in our time and place, we must "make time" for them. Ignoring the opportunity to intentionally incorporate Christian-based films as a potential spiritual discipline to support spiritual growth and deepen our relationship with Jesus Christ, would be regrettable to the process of spiritual formation. Exploring God's storytelling along with homiletics professor Kenley D. Hall, I assert that God has chosen to use stories to reveal God's self and as an emotionally invested way to communicate with humanity.[15] Jesus' parables cast a vision on the imaginations of those who were open to seeing the story being told and experiencing

---

12. Higgins, "Film Criticism as Spiritual Discipline."
13. John 14:12.
14. Higgins, *How Movies Helped Saved My Soul*, 255.
15. Hall, "Jesus, God's Story and Storyteller."

the transformation that resulted in salvation and reconciliation with God.[16] Moreover, the Holy Spirit amplifies the work of Jesus through those who believe in him in various ways throughout history, in our present time, and with unlimited possibilities in the future.

In other words, in our present-day context, instructing people to read their Bibles and pay attention to the sermon on Sunday morning is not enough. We must consider how films engage people in popular culture to help them remember what they need to know about God, the Scriptures, the Gospel of Jesus Christ, and the way to eternal life. Acknowledging and incorporating screen stories can play a vital role in helping others connect and bring understanding to their faith journey. As we will see, God has created us with imagination and an attraction to storytelling—a fact attested to in a vast number of spiritual, neuroscientific, psychological, and emotional studies. Such scholarship undergirds my contention that films can be an indispensable way to connect with God, understand God, and grow closer to God.

Indeed, Christian-based films are an opportunity to discern beyond the screen and discover the spiritual formation being activated within us and among us in all three scenarios. The central argument claim addresses how storytelling through Christian-based films has the potential to be used as a spiritual discipline to bring us to spiritual maturity in our spiritual formation journey. Visual arts and the ingenuity the genre offers in reaching people spiritually, psychologically, and informatively need to be explored and presented as a resource for spiritual formation. As a spiritual discipline, the storytelling media genre can stimulate an internal response to nurture disciples and make more disciples as Christ commissioned. The purpose of this book, then, is to provide a practical understanding of how Christian-based films have the potential to be practiced as a spiritual discipline for spiritual growth and to cultivate a deeper relationship with Jesus Christ. Through my research findings and analysis, I will provide an account of the spiritual and film formation foundations along with spiritual discipleship strategies to use visual media in spiritual formation.

To do this, I first examine the traditional spiritual disciplines and their roles in spiritual formation. Next, I show how the example of Jesus as a master storyteller should serve as a paradigm for all those who seek to make disciples in Christ's name and lead others into a deeper relationship with God through the power of the Holy Spirit. Then, through a brief

---

16. Hall, "Jesus, God's Story and Storyteller," 13.

INTRODUCTION

recounting of cinema's history and the distinctive formal elements of film as a medium, I begin to show how film media can be a tool for spiritual, moral, and ethical formation in influencing and engaging popular culture. Finally, I provide a case study of three movies, *A Question of Faith*, *Soul Surfer*, and *Son of God*. Through assessing these three films, I explore distinct Christian-based themes emphasized in their storytelling and demonstrate how they address life issues that can lead to spiritual growth.

EXTENDED OUTLINE

To accomplish this task, chapter 1 provides a general overview of spiritual formation and the purpose of the traditional spiritual disciplines in the process of spiritual maturity. Here, I detail what the spiritual disciplines are, why we need them in our spiritual formation, and how they contribute to our spiritual growth as disciples of Jesus Christ. The spiritual discipline foundation will provide the necessary framework for potentially approaching Christian-based films as a comparable spiritual growth tool in spiritual formation.

Chapter 2 addresses God's use of storytelling and how the art of storytelling has evolved into visual media. Storytelling through movies has been a way of engaging, understanding, coping, and healing for others and myself throughout my ministry, and storytelling has been a means to pass on faith traditions, historical information, and moral values throughout time. The function of the method is unsurprising once we recognize that storytelling was how Jesus captured and kept an audience while illuminating his point in his preaching and teaching. Parables were a creative way to tap into imagination, connect with internal emotions, and illustrate spiritual lessons. Likewise, imaginative stories continue to be a means to convey, teach, and understand the Gospel of Jesus Christ. Christian-based films and television programming are constantly created and shared worldwide, offering opportunities for spiritual introspection to bring about spiritual growth to witness creatively. Ultimately, the central argument claim seeks to provide a practical understanding of Christian-based film as modern-day parables or storytelling that can function as a spiritual discipline in a person's spiritual formation. Cinema's ingenuity and unique capacity to minister to people and support spiritual growth must be explored intentionally and presented as a resource for spiritual formation.

The goal of chapter 3 is to provide a foundational understanding of the historical, theological, ecclesial, cultural, and spiritual influences cinema has had on our society from its inception. By examining cinema's longstanding influence and the power movies continue to have through its distinctive formal properties, we can develop a deeper understanding of how the particular dynamics of movies lend the opportunity for spiritual formation and discipleship. (Throughout the book, I will interchangeably refer to films using terms such as cinema, movies, motion pictures, and screen stories, reflecting various perspectives on the genre. "Screen stories" is the term that Carl Plantinga uses to describe films.)[17]

Drawing together the accumulated insights regarding spiritual formation, the nature of storytelling, and cinema's ongoing role in shaping culture, I then make a specific case for Christian-based films as a potential spiritual discipline tool in spiritual formation by assessing three Christian-based films. Chapter 4 uses three movies, *A Question of Faith*, *Soul Surfer*, and *Son of God*, as case studies to demonstrate in more detail how Christian-based films have the potential to influence viewers who engage the genre as a spiritual discipline. As part of the analysis, I provide a framework to model a possible avenue of how the Holy Spirit works through films as storytelling to share the Gospel of Jesus Christ and guide us in discerning beyond the screen. Embracing the process has the potential to lead us to a response of transcendence and transformation that brings spiritual growth and a deeper relationship with Jesus Christ.

In conclusion, I will reiterate how film as storytelling is a method that God may use to have an encounter with viewers and communicate the Gospel and teachings of Jesus Christ. Through the process of surrender and discernment to the Holy Spirit's use of Christian-based films in our spiritual formation, we can grow and deepen our relationship with Jesus Christ. I reiterate the need to intentionally engage Christian-based films as a spiritual discipline with a posture of prayer and discernment. In the process, the ultimate objective is to have the eyes to see and the ears to hear what the Holy Spirit is communicating to advance our spiritual growth and the Gospel of Jesus Christ in bringing us to spiritual maturity and making more disciples.

---

17. See Plantinga, *Screen Stories*.

Chapter One

Spiritual Formation

CHRISTIAN-BASED FILMS AND TELEVISION programming are flourishing and shared worldwide, offering opportunities for spiritual introspection to bring about spiritual growth and engage discipleship creatively.[1] Thus, my central argument seeks to demonstrate that by intentionally integrating Christian-based movies and shows, faith leaders can encourage members of their communities to initiate, establish, grow, and sustain a relationship with Jesus Christ. In presenting the claim mentioned above, I will examine the influence of Christian-based storytelling dramatized through movies, potentially impacting viewers' Christian spiritual formation. I will also explore how modern-day storytelling through visual media can likewise be a powerful tool as a spiritual discipline as an ongoing method of spiritual growth and nurturing a deeper relationship with Jesus Christ.

The primary pillar in support of my claim is establishing a general understanding of spiritual formation and spiritual disciplines. Determining what a spiritual discipline is and its purpose in our spiritual development will solidify Christian-based films' inclusion within the category. Broadly speaking, Christian spiritual formation refers to the process of encouraging spiritual growth and deepening a relationship with Jesus Christ. One of its foundational tenets is the practice of spiritual disciplines. Spiritual disciplines are the methods the Body of Christ consistently exercises to align with Jesus and how he taught disciples to live an abundant life and as

---

1. Movieguide, "Movies with Strong Christian Content Are Flourishing."

salt and light in the world.² What follows is a more detailed examination of traditional spiritual disciplines, aiming to deepen our understanding of how viewing Christian-based films might work similarly and towards the same goal: life more abundantly in Jesus Christ.

WHAT IS SPIRITUAL FORMATION AND WHAT ARE SPIRITUAL DISCIPLINES?

Spiritual Formation

I distinctly remember the moment I was asked the question, "How do you define spiritual formation?" I was sitting in the spiritual formation course I was required to take in seminary for my Master of Divinity degree. In an attempt to answer the question with no prior formal definition presented to me for the concept, I recall responding that spiritual formation was the process of becoming more like Jesus Christ. The professor did not indicate that I had missed the mark in defining the term, but I came to understand some details that I needed to include in my definition.

Christian scholar, philosopher, and author Dallas Willard has been a primary source for understanding what spiritual formation is and is not. Some of his teachings on spiritual formation are found on the website dedicated to his work. Willard defines spiritual formation extensively, citing Old Testament Scripture Proverbs 4:20–24 and New Testament Scriptures Mark 7:15, 20–23, and Luke 6:43–45.³ These Scriptures speak to the wisdom of God in our hearts, emphasizing the importance of guarding our hearts, as what is in our hearts flows out into our actions.⁴

Willard elaborates on the progression of spiritual formation in the New Testament, grounding his teachings in 2 Peter 1:4–7.⁵ He explains what being grafted into Jesus means for followers, who should emulate Christ. Additionally, Willard highlights Colossians 3:14 and Romans 5:5, emphasizing that agape (love) will be evident as spiritual formation progresses.⁶ Willard indeed has had an enormous influence on the world of understanding spiritual formation and is instrumental in how I understand

---

2. Willard, *The Spirit of the Disciplines*, 86–145.
3. Willard, "Spiritual Formation," para 2-3.
4. Willard, "Spiritual Formation," para 2-4.
5. Willard, "Spiritual Formation," para 6.
6. Willard, "Spiritual Formation," para 7.

the need to consider incorporating Christian-based films as a possible spiritual discipline tool.

The following offers a definition and key descriptions of spiritual formation in Willard's own words:

> Spiritual formation in the tradition of Jesus Christ is the process of transformation of the inmost dimension of the human being, the heart, which is the same as the spirit or will. It is being formed (really, transformed) in such a way that its natural expression comes to be the deeds of Christ done in the power of Christ.[7]
>
> When we talk about spiritual formation we are talking about framing a progression of life in which people come to actually do all things that Jesus taught. So we are obviously going for the heart. We are aiming for change of the inner person, where what we do originates.[8]
>
> Christian spiritual formation is the process through which the embodied/reflective will takes on the character of Christ's will. It is the process through which (and you know Gal. 4:19) Christ is formed in you and me.[9]
>
> Spiritual formation in Christ would, then, ideally result in a person whose reflective will for good, fully informed and possessed by Christ, has settled into their body in its social context to such an extent that their natural responses were always to think and feel and do as Christ himself would.[10]

Willard offers a wealth of information for persons seeking to understand what spiritual formation means and how the idea of spiritual formation evolved. He also shares the dangers to spiritual formation brought on by "new age" spirituality that focuses more on the formation of self rather than being formed into Christlikeness. For Willard, a crucial criterion for practicing and progressing in spiritual formation is found in John 15:5 where Jesus told his disciples that the spiritual work within them (and, by implication, us) would not be accomplished without him.[11] No matter what spiritual discipline we choose to practice, spiritual formation must be the work of the Holy Spirit, processing the transformation within us. That is,

---

7. Willard, "Spiritual Formation," para 5.
8. Willard, "Spiritual Formation," para 31.
9. Willard, "Spiritual Formation," para 40.
10. Willard, "Spiritual Formation," para 46.
11. Willard, "Spiritual Formation," para 9.

any worthwhile understanding of spiritual formation must prioritize and emphasize the work of the Holy Spirit.

Crucially for my core idea, Dallas Willard provides an understanding of spiritual formation that gives insight into how Christian-based screen stories can be a spiritual discipline in spiritual formation. For a practice to align with the work of spiritual formation, the work must result in influencing a transcendent response of transformation into the likeness of Christ. I will share more about films' powerful influence in chapter 3. Again, the work of the Holy Spirit in the process is to be held close to the vest as a reminder that we are not transforming ourselves by sitting before a screen searching for Christian meaning, lessons, encouragement, or even wholesome entertainment. Before I address how films contribute to spiritual formation as a possible spiritual discipline, it is vital to know why we need spiritual disciplines and their contribution to spiritual growth. In doing so, I will later show how Christian-based films can be a spiritual discipline and how the traditional disciplines are also expressed collaboratively through Christian-based films.

Spiritual Disciplines

Much like Willard, the Renovaré Institute for Christian Spiritual Formation defines spiritual formation as "a process, but it is also a journey through which we open our hearts to a deeper connection with God. We are not bystanders in our spiritual lives, we are active participants with God, who is ever inviting us into relationship with him."[12]

As I further provide the foundation for spiritual formation, Richard J. Foster, the author of *Celebration of Discipline* and founder of the Renovaré Institute of Christian Spiritual Formation USA, continues to be instrumental in developing authentic Christocentric communities. *Celebration of Discipline* was my formal introduction to the practice of the classic spiritual disciplines and how to accomplish what Willard emphasizes as the intentional work we must do in spiritual formation.

Like Dallas Willard, the Renovaré Institute provides a deeper understanding of spiritual formation, even quoting Willard when expounding on the practice in Scripture by saying, "'Repent, for the kingdom of the heavens is at hand' (Matt 3:2, 4:17, 10:7). This is a call for us to reconsider how we have been approaching our life, in light of the fact that we now,

12. Renovaré, "Spiritual Formation," para 2.

in the presence of Jesus, have the option of living within the surrounding movements of God's eternal purposes, of taking our life into his life."[13]

Renovaré Institute is a Christian nonprofit that models, resources, and advocates fullness of life with God experienced by grace through the spiritual practices of Jesus and of the historical Church.[14] The Renovaré Institute emphasizes that the Bible provides solid support for spiritual formation and includes scriptural references with classic spiritual disciplines. Spiritual disciplines are integral to spiritual development because they stretch, mold, and equip us to walk in the ways Jesus exemplified and commanded His followers to model. The Renovaré Institute and Richard Foster offer the following definition for spiritual disciplines: "the practices of Jesus have been recognized for centuries as the core activities of the spiritual life."[15]

However, their definition of spiritual disciplines limits how Jesus may seek to relate to and reach the fast, technologically advancing generations of the twenty-first century. As Dallas Willard says, "a discipline for the spiritual life is, when the dust of history is blown away, nothing but an activity undertaken to bring us into more effective cooperation with Christ and his Kingdom."[16] Willard explains that spiritual disciplines are the exercises or activities that enable us to receive more of Christ and his power without harming ourselves or others.[17] He goes on to say, "when we understand that grace (charis) is gift (charisma), we then see that to grow in grace is to grow in what is given to us of God and by God."[18] The reference to the training tools previously mentioned in the Scriptures that Willard lists for spiritual transformation is expounded in our understanding of the spiritual disciplines.

The main premise of this book argues for the possibility of embracing film as a gracious gift, "given to us of God and by God." Christian-based movies fulfill the mandate by dramatizing storytelling, sharing "more of Christ and his power" while showing the impact of what a life with or without Christ may produce through an influential platform. Some may debate whether Christian-based films are spiritually beneficial or potentially cause

---

13. Renovaré, "Spiritual Formation," para 9.
14. Renovaré Institute, "Overview."
15. Renovaré Institute, "Spiritual Disciplines," para 2.
16. Willard, *Spirit of the Disciplines*, 156.
17. Willard, *Spirit of the Disciplines*, 156.
18. Willard, *Spirit of the Disciplines*, 156. *Charis* is the Greek for grace; it is also the root for the word "charisma."

more significant harm by the theology communicated in some movies. I will address the conflicting views in more detail in chapter 3 and discuss how discernment is critical in choosing films for spiritual formation purposes. However, as Willard explains spiritual disciplines, his definition opens the door for Christian-based films, as a growing gift of grace from God, to be added as a practical activity to experience spiritual formation.

Indeed, going to the movies or streaming movies on personal devices is one of today's most common and popular cultural activities. Some people will watch more movies and television than they will ever pick up a Bible to read, attend a church service in their lifetime, or practice most of the traditional spiritual disciplines that Foster historically references. Recognizing the trends displayed in popular culture that demonstrate a steady move away from finding spirituality in churches, Christian leaders must adapt to discovering ways of efficacy to equip believers and reach new disciples.[19] To be clear, in no way does this imply that the traditional spiritual disciplines are irrelevant or unnecessary. Nevertheless, a "traditioned innovation" approach to introduce, teach, and fuel the fire to practice the disciplines must be considered.[20] The Holy Spirit will meet us in our efforts, and we will experience the growth in grace resulting in the gift of spiritual transformation. As Willard explains in his commentary on the foundational Scripture of 2 Peter 1:5–8:

> Though we may not be aware of it, we experience 'disciplines' everyday. In these daily or 'natural' disciplines we perform acts that result in a direct command of further abilities that we would not otherwise have. . .Such ordinary activities are actually disciplines that aid our physical or 'natural' life. The same thing happens with disciplines for our spiritual life. When through spiritual disciplines I become able heartily to bless those who curse me, pray without ceasing, to be at peace when not given credit for good deeds I've done, or to master the evil that comes my way, it is because my disciplinary activities have inwardly poised me for more and more interaction with the powers of the living God and his Kingdom. Such is the potential we tap into when we use the disciplines.[21]

Despite what might be considered an overemphasis on the "traditional disciplines," Foster agrees with Willard regarding grace's role in the spiritual

---

19. Johnston, et al., *Deep Focus*, 39.
20. Faith and Leadership, "Traditioned Innovation."
21. Willard, *Spirit of the Disciplines*, 156.

discipline process. He describes the spiritual disciplines as opening a door that gives way to the gift of God offered through inner transformation.[22] Clearly echoing Willard, Foster reiterates:

> When we despair of gaining inner transformation through human powers of will and determination, we are open to a wonderful new realization: inner righteousness is a gift from God to be graciously received. The needed change within us is God's work, not ours. The demand is for an inside job, and only God can work from the inside. We cannot attain or earn this righteousness of the kingdom of God; it is a grace that is given.[23]

I agree with Willard and Foster in the working of God in us. But I would be even more specific and reiterate the work of the Holy Spirit in us doing the work. The Holy Spirit is the one Jesus said would teach us, remind us of everything he has said, lead us to all truth, and help us live in alignment as disciples of Christ. Jesus promised in John 14:16–26 that the Holy Spirit's purpose is to be with us, guide us in the spiritual transformation process, and be our "weight spotter" as we are in spiritual training. A weight-spotter is someone who supports another person while they are doing a particular exercise such as weight-lifting. The Holy Spirit is the help that Jesus promised we would receive as believers (John 14:16). Reemphasizing the staple of the Holy Spirit here is necessary for the transformational work anticipated for those who choose Christian-based screen stories as a spiritual discipline in their spiritual formation process. Moving away from understanding the Holy Spirit's crucial role has the potential for viewers to engage in watching just another film for entertainment purposes only.

Laying a foundation of what the spiritual disciplines mean and their purpose in our lives is necessary for supporting my central argument to potentially incorporate Christian-based films into the practice. The classic spiritual disciplines are an essential entity of spiritual formation. The understanding and practice of traditional spiritual disciplines should serve as a standard for integrating Christian-based films into spiritual formation. Although there needs to be consideration given to how to integrate Christian-based films as a viable spiritual discipline, I am careful not to throw the baby out with the bath water. I can build Christian-based films as a potential spiritual discipline on the traditional foundation by examining the classic spiritual disciplines. The classics are necessities to live freely and

---

22. Foster, *Celebration of Discipline*, 5.
23. Foster, *Celebration of Discipline*, 5.

experience the abundant life that Jesus promises those who follow him. According to Richard Foster, the inward, outward, and corporate disciplines in *Celebration of Discipline* are classic spiritual disciplines. These are the disciplines that most Christian scholars, theologians, preachers, and teachers identify as the traditional disciplines we engage in, most commonly as individuals and as a community of believers in Jesus Christ. Foster details the twelve traditional (inward, outward, and corporate) disciplines in his book. We will find each discipline highlighted in Scripture and practiced in the Old and New Testaments of the Holy Bible.

Inward Disciplines

Foster's book lists inward disciplines as meditation, prayer, fasting, and study.[24] When considering the inward disciplines, the spiritual formation work is a personal experience that typically happens between the Triune God and an individual. We receive the inward spiritual disciplines as the introspective training necessary for the Holy Spirit to transform our hearts, minds, and spirits. The inward disciplines are foundational to understanding Christian-based films to be utilized as a spiritual discipline because of the work necessary for individuals to discern what the Holy Spirit is communicating to them through the screen stories. As we meditate, pray, fast, and study, the message can and, by faith, will move us into discerning the spiritual revelations concerning our lives and draw us nearer to Jesus Christ. Furthermore, spiritual disciplines are often displayed collaboratively in many Christian-based films dramatizing what practicing the disciplines looks like for viewers. Using movies to introduce and teach disciples spiritual disciplines is an innovative way to equip them outside traditional church settings.

Outward Disciplines

According to Foster, the outward disciplines are training tools that strengthen our preparation to sustain the inward disciplines practiced. Foster lists the outward disciplines as simplicity, solitude, submission, and service. The outward disciplines are also foundational to understanding Christian-based films as a potential spiritual discipline. The outward disciplines train

---

24. Foster, *Celebration of Discipline*.

us to recognize and release the distractions around us and give ourselves to fully be present with what is before us and what we need to accomplish. Moreover, we are able to posture ourselves in a place of discerning the Presence of God within us and among us. As I introduce Christian-based films as a possible spiritual discipline, moving beyond internal and external distractions will be vital to discerning beyond the screen to submit to the work of the Holy Spirit in growing and sustaining our spiritual growth.

Corporate Disciplines

Foster's final tier of spiritual disciplines is the corporate disciplines, which include the practices of confession, worship, guidance, and celebration. The times we gather together with other disciples of Christ and experience the community of "iron sharpening iron" result from the corporate disciplines.[25] We need each other and move from the personal work of spiritual transformation with the Holy Spirit to the family of disciples of Christ, glorifying God and edifying each other.

In that context, using Christian-based films as a spiritual discipline tool is an ideal fit as a corporate discipline. Traditionally, people have gathered together as a community to watch the latest feature in the movie theater. Churches have increasingly sought to host fellowship gatherings at the movie theaters or turn their sanctuaries or parking lots into community theaters for Christian and non-Christian family appropriate movie screenings. The Body of Christ has figured out that gathering for films and showing films at their places of worship provides a less intimidating environment for fellowship that can lead to confession, worship, guidance, celebration, and expressions of the inward and outward disciplines.

Incorporating the traditional spiritual disciplines into disciples' lives requires identifying and laying the foundation for the core idea claim of adding Christian-based films to the list of disciplines. More importantly, as I substantiate the claim, I agree with Willard when he says, "the aim and substance of spiritual life is not fasting, prayer, hymn singing, frugal living, and so forth. Rather, it is the effective and full enjoyment of active love of God and humankind in all the daily rounds of normal existence where we are placed."[26] In Willard's words, I am reminded of Brother Lawrence and how he looked for, expected, and found the presence of God in everything

---

25. Ps 27:17 (NIV) states, "as iron sharpens iron, so one person sharpens another."
26. Willard, *The Spirit of the Disciplines*, 137.

he did.[27] Film is among the "daily rounds of normal existence where we are placed" and is a valuable tool that is not absent of God's awareness or lacking as a means of spiritual growth or salvation.

LAYING A FOUNDATION FOR PERSONAL AND COMMUNITY SPIRITUAL FORMATION

Jesus Christ is the example of how believers are to live a life that seeks to align with God. We gain insight into spiritual formation by intentionally examining how Jesus cultivated a relationship with God, The Father, and humanity. Studying Jesus' relationship with his Father and how Jesus related to humanity is a guide to developing inward, outward, and corporate spiritual disciplines and how to be equipped for discipleship. To confine God to our finite structures and meaning of spiritual development is a barrier to reaching people for Christ, blocking a path that Jesus has opened up for so many people to find him and receive the gift of salvation that comes through him. We must find innovative ways to disciple in a world that has consistently moved away from the Christian church as the best spiritual and foundational moral choice. We have ended up in an unfamiliar discipleship conundrum because of polarizing issues like political compromise, ethical disgraces, and judgmental spirits. As Jesus commands us in the Great Commission, "Therefore go and make disciples of all nations, baptizing them in the name of the Father and of the Son and of the Holy Spirit, and teaching them to obey everything I have commanded you. And surely I am with you always, to the very end of the age," we need to discover the best ways to reach people for discipleship.[28] How did Jesus get to the hearts of the people who engaged him? Where are the places in Scripture when we find Jesus in places religious practitioners did not go or thought they should not be? Jesus sat in the company of sinners wherever he needed to gather with them. Are we not to consider and do the same?

The Apostle Paul offers us an understanding of Jesus' principle of presence and discipleship in 1 Corinthians 9:

> Though I am free and belong to no one, I have made myself a slave to everyone, to win as many as possible. To the Jews I became like a Jew, to win the Jews. To those under the law I became like one

---

27. Brother Lawrence, *The Practice of the Presence of God*.
28. Matt 28:19–20 (NIV).

under the law (though I myself am not under the law), so as to win those under the law. To those not having the law I became like one not having the law (though I am not free from God's law but am under Christ's law), so as to win those not having the law. To the weak I became weak, to win the weak. I have become all things to all people so that by all possible means I might save some. I do all this for the sake of the gospel, that I may share in its blessings.[29]

In *Learning from Jesus: A Spiritual Formation Guide*, Lynda L. Graybeal and Julia L. Roller note that one obstacle in our spiritual formation growth may be in our traditions. Not everyone is willing to take the spiritual posterity of Paul and be all to save all for the sake of Christ. However, various traditions agree that being formed into Christlikeness is a necessity.

> While many Christian traditions differ over the details of spiritual formation, they all come out at the same place: the transformation of the person into Christlikeness. 'Spiritual formation' is the process of transforming the inner reality of the self. . .in such a way that the overall life with God seen in Bible naturally and freely comes to pass in us. Our inner world (the secret heart) becomes the home of Jesus, by his initiative and our response. As a result, our interior world becomes increasingly like the inner self Jesus and, therefore, the natural source of words and deeds that are characteristic of him. By his enabling presence, we come to "let the same mind be in you that was in Christ Jesus" (Phil 2:5).[30]

While Christian traditions may vary, if the approach to spiritual formation mirrors the mind of Christ and the openness of Paul, methods such as Christian-based films can be incorporated into the realm of spiritual disciplines.

To consider incorporating Christian-based films as a possible spiritual discipline, Renovaré Institute provides a deeper insight into the freedom God offers through Christ Jesus in having an abundant life. The Renovaré website shares three statements that help solidify thoughts concerning the central argument claim:

> Jesus said, "I came that they may have life and have it abundantly" (John 10:10). We at Renovaré believe that such abundant life is possible here and now because Jesus showed us the way to it. As we take on the life of Jesus—become like him—we experience

---

29. 1 Cor 9:19–23 (NIV).
30. Graybeal and Roller, *Learning from Jesus*, xii–xiii.

> a richness in life and faith that is truly renewed day by day (Col 3:10).
>
> Closeness with God brings us true freedom and fullness (John 8:36, Col 2:9–10). Yet many people—Christians included—find their lives fall short of the kind Jesus promised and proclaimed. If God is present with us, why is there so little joy, power, energy, and peace in our lives?
>
> ... Spiritual formation helps us reclaim our relationship with God as it was meant to be. It's not trying—it's training in eternal living, determined discipleship to Jesus Christ, and the way we discover the renewable source of spiritual energy we've been looking for (2 Cor 4:16).[31]

What does abundant life look like for followers of Christ? How do we know when we are living an abundant life? If God is present with us always and the earth is the Lord's and everything in it, why do people tend to place restrictions on God?[32] How often do people, specifically Christians, put God in a box with a list of dos, don'ts, cans, can'ts, musts, and nevers that keep God from moving in the lives of believers and seekers?

The previous questions prompt me to think of when Jesus denounced the Pharisees and Scribes in the New Testament for the standards they held people to that they could not keep themselves. Consider the statement Jesus made to those he called hypocrites:

> Woe to you, teachers of the law and Pharisees, you hypocrites! You shut the door of the kingdom of heaven in people's faces. You yourselves do not enter, nor will you let those enter who are trying to. Woe to you, teachers of the law and Pharisees, you hypocrites! You travel over land and sea to win a single convert, and when you have succeeded, you make them twice as much a child of hell as you are.[33]

If we do not intentionally consider how films can be a tool that the Holy Spirit uses to guide us in the training process of spiritual formation, we risk becoming like the charlatans Jesus identified—those who lock people out of the doors to the kingdom of heaven.

Given all of this, one could argue that any practice can be considered a spiritual discipline. Considering interests such as reading a novel, painting

---

31. Renovaré, "Spiritual Formation," para 4, 8.
32. Ps 24:1 (NRSVUE).
33. Matt 23:13–15 (NIV).

Spiritual Formation

a portrait, or cooking a meal could be among the list of practices. Suppose those practices fit the definition of a spiritual discipline to support spiritual growth and deepen our relationship with Jesus Christ. In that case, substantiating the claim when making the argument requires laying a foundation that supports the goal of a spiritual discipline. Clearly, some overlooked, underappreciated, and never considered possible spiritual disciplines are available to practice in accomplishing our spiritual development goals. Engaging Christian-based films as a potential spiritual discipline is one of those entities I am claiming as the central argument. We live in the twenty-first century, and society has changed from sermons on the mountainside to messages preached on television and social media platforms that present reasonable Christocentric practices not in Scripture. However, the purpose and intent are the same: to share the Good News of the Gospel of Jesus Christ and teach how to live a life as disciples of Christ.

Jesus told stories and parables to capture the attention and hearts of his listeners to share what life in him looked like, would feel like, and bring to the believer. Some of Jesus' most notable stories are the Parable of the Prodigal Son, the Parable of the Good Samaritan, and the Parable of the Talents. Jesus creatively engaged the thoughts of those who heard the stories to bring awareness to places in their lives that needed clarity and change. Screen stories align with Jesus' methods to reach people's hearts seeking to engage their imaginations and spiritually transform them. Over a thousand years ago, films did not exist. However, screen stories have become the evolution of storytelling for those who would be intrigued by Jesus' masterful storytelling during the time he walked the earth.

Robert K. Johnston, professor and theologian of film and culture argues that movies are equipped with the same technique as parables to unpredictably trigger viewers' imaginations to see the possible outcomes for themselves and others dramatized on a screen.[34] Thus, Johnston adds weight to the central argument that Christian-based films can be a spiritual discipline. He acknowledges how movies "help viewers to see life more clearly," "catch us off guard and tell us things about ourselves and others," and lead to a transformational response.[35] In follow-up, Johnston says, "viewed in this light, movies are part of the toolbox that many people use as they respond to and give shape to their lives. As such, they can be a

---

34. Johnston, *Reel Spirituality*, 64.
35. Johnston, Reel Spirituality, 64.

significant ingredient in a person's individual formation."[36] The next chapter will assess Jesus' use of storytelling and the powerful influence of storytelling through Christian-based films that can accomplish the goal of a spiritual discipline in developing spiritual formation.

36. Johnston, Reel Spirituality, 64.

Chapter Two

Storytelling, Parables, and Christian-based Films' Significance in Spiritual Formation

STORYTELLING IS A FUNDAMENTAL part of how we come to know God and understand God's relationship to humanity. It is how we are interconnected to God's salvific plan. If spiritual formation and discipleship are the processes of connecting with God and being conformed to the image of Christ through the help of the Holy Spirit, then engaging the story of God is how we come to understand who God is. In turn, as we build a relationship and intimacy with God by believing God's redemptive story, we have a command from Jesus Christ to share The Gospel with others so that they may also believe in God and God's plan of salvation.

In Deuteronomy 11:18–21, God gives a command to the Israelites to put the words (commands) that the Lord had spoken on their hearts and souls, hands and foreheads, doorposts and gates, and to tell them to their children. The generations were to know the story of God's command so that they would know God, understand God's expectations, and live out what God required of them. In Matthew 28:19–20, Jesus gives The Great Commission to the disciples (Apostles) to go make more disciples by telling all nations about what he had taught them. To share the Gospel and make disciples, the story of Jesus and his message would have to be told. The spiritual formation process is a discipleship pipeline, and storytelling is one of the primary tools by which the mandate to share is carried out throughout history.

The first step in making disciples is becoming one. Becoming a disciple of Jesus Christ is to believe in who he is as the Savior, embrace his teachings, and follow his way to salvation. As we become disciples, we have a calling to fulfill Jesus' mandate to make more disciples by teaching or sharing what he has taught with the help of the Holy Spirit. The methods of becoming disciples and making disciples may look different for each of us in how the teachings of Jesus came into our lives and how we share The Gospel with others. If storytelling is a tool used to make disciples by sharing the Gospel of Jesus Christ, then Christian-based screen stories are among the genre of storytelling. They can be further considered a spiritual discipline as a tool used to cultivate spiritual growth and a deeper relationship with Jesus Christ.

WHAT IS STORYTELLING?

According to the authors of *Research Through, With and As Storying*, Louise Gwenneth Phillips and Tracey Bunda, story is "the communication of what it means to be human, that tells of emplaced, relational tragedies, challenges and joys of living. Stories are spoken, gestured, danced, dramatized, painted, drawn, etched, sculpted, woven, stitched, filmed, written and any combination of these modes and more."[1] When we turn on the news or read an article, we are told a story by a storyteller. Conversations with others often involve some form of storytelling. When we go to church and participate in worship or listen to a sermon, we experience a story being told about God and our connection to God. In reading or listening to the Holy Bible, we are introduced to God and engage in the narrative of God creating the heavens, the earth, human beings, and the plan for our existence. Storytelling has a role in all of our lives. Whether those stories have been fact or fiction, oral, written, or visual, and for our knowledge or entertainment, none of us have experienced life without the influence of storytelling. Observing that storytelling is interwoven into the fibers of humanity, consideration is given to 1) God's purpose in using storytelling to connect with us and 2) how films fit into the scheme of God's storytelling plan.

---

1. Phillips and Bunda, *Research Through*, 3.

STORYTELLING, PARABLES, AND CHRISTIAN-BASED FILMS'

WHY STORYING?

Storytelling has been used to record history, pass on generational traditions, entertain, share news reports, witness the details of our faith, and communicate the story of God and the message of salvation through Jesus Christ. In his work in ethics and storytelling, theologian Stanley Hauerwas says: "metaphors and stories entice us to find a way to bring into existence the reality that at once should be but will not be except as we act as if it is. Morally the world is always wanting to be created in correspondence to what it is but is not yet."[2] That is, beyond being a means of entertainment or historical record, stories make sense of our lives and the world. In doing so, there may be factual representation, while at other times, fiction development is infused by our imaginations. In the ethical sense, Hauerwas recommends that the metaphors and stories we develop can provide guidance to living with integrity.[3] As Carl Plantinga asserts, stories are "integral to the formation of our social identities."[4]

Homiletics Professor Kenley D. Hall says that stories and images drive postmodern society.[5] His insight comes from focusing on the Millennials and Gen Zers who "talk in story" as they live in a world consumed with social media, which is their everyday norm of communication and expression.[6] As our present and future generations engage story, there is a search for the truth and for that truth to be interactive and engaging. I would add that many of the people who live in our world today who have technology readily available to them do not just "talk in story," but they are eagerly searching and viewing stories through social media, streaming platforms, and communication icons such as texting emojis. Hall concludes by saying that our brains are wired to respond to and crave stories, and we have an innate ability to tell stories.[7] Whether the evolution of storying is considered positive, negative, or both, depending on its contribution to truth or deception, our society gravitates toward storytelling as a premier way to communicate personally, professionally, academically, socially, and spiritually.

---

2. Berkman and Cartwright, *The Hauerwas Reader*, 168.
3. Berkman and Cartwright, *The Hauerwas Reader*, 169.
4. Plantinga, "The Power of Screen Stories," 12.
5. Hall, "Jesus, God's Story and Storyteller," 10.
6. Hall, "Jesus, God's Story and Storyteller," 10.
7. Hall, "Jesus, God's Story and Storyteller," 13.

The adage, "Like Father, Like Son," has been a saying through generations to explain similar characteristics or behaviors between parents and their children. The same sentiment comes to mind when seeking to understand why we tell stories and are fascinated by storytelling in various forms. I connect the adage to how God created us in the Imago Dei. The desirability of storying is in our DNA and leads to humanity being, "Like Creator, Like Creation." As humankind is indeed made in the image of God and God is a storyteller, then we, too, innately live our lives as storytellers like Elohim, our Creator.

Again, we come to know God through the story of God. When we consider the sermons that are preached, the Bible study lessons that are taught, and the worship services that we attend, all of these spiritual acts tell a story about God and our interaction with God. For Christians, the story begins with Genesis, has a middle narrative of redemption through Christ, and ends with a promise of the Parousia of Christ in Revelation. However, the story continues because humanity is still living out our relationship with God and each other. As humanity lives on until the Second Coming of Christ, we will persist in storytelling, and our storytelling will continue to evolve. Christian-based screen stories are among the evolution of storytelling that has the power to influence a diverse world.

THE DIVINE STORYTELLER: BIBLICAL STORYING, PARABLES, AND JESUS' METHODS OF STORYTELLING

"God is the greatest storyteller ever. Our most brilliant, most captivating, most spellbinding authors have nothing in comparison to the Lord's storytelling abilities. All good stories are but pale reflections and imitations of the great story of God's glory brought to bear in the world," is how pastor, professor, and author Jared C. Wilson describes God as the Master Storyteller.[8] Storytelling was a way Jesus captured an audience while illuminating his point in his preaching and teaching. The method of storytelling that is most popularly associated with Jesus is speaking in parables. A parable is a "usually short fictitious story that illustrates a moral attitude or a religious principle."[9] To better understand the meaning of a parable in the context and use of Jesus as a method of storytelling, the Hebrew word associated

---

8. Wilson, *The Storytelling God*, 21.
9. Merriam-Webster.com Dictionary, s.v. "parable."

with parable is mashal which means "comparison."[10] Wilson highlights the Greek meaning of parable: "to cast alongside."[11] In considering parables as a model for how Christian-based films can be a spiritual discipline, the Encyclopedia of the Bible seems especially helpful: "A parable is a saying or story that seeks to drive home a point the speaker wishes to emphasize by illustrating it from a familiar situation of common life."[12]

One of the most transformative parables in God's story shared in the Old Testament is the convicting encounter between David and Nathan in 2 Samuel 12. The Scripture tells us the story of when David should have been away at war with his soldiers but stayed behind, only to end up committing a sin by having an affair with his soldier's (Uriah) wife, Bathsheba. When we read the account of how the parable opened David's spiritual eyes to his indiscretions, we see the transcendent power of the story in his transformative response that led to repentance.[13]

Wilson describes a particularly sensitive situation: "The prophet [. . .] understands the delicacy in rebuking the king for his sin. In an interesting turn of events, the subtle use of parable actually has a more powerful effect than an outright rebuke might have accomplished."[14] Undoubtedly, the Spirit of The Lord gave Nathan the inspiration for the parable. Through the use of storying, God gave the prophet Nathan a method to reach David's dulled heart caused by his sinful acts of lust, adultery, deception, murder, and a cover-up. The parable caused David's visual imagination to see beyond himself to discern what was right and wrong in the story's message. David was so deep in the dark that a light of revelation needed to shine into the space he no longer had the sight to see concerning his own life. Once Nathan delivered the parable, David was faced with the truth of his own transgressions and was convicted.

Likewise, as we navigate through the complexities of our lives, the decisions we make, and the spiritual blindness we often experience, God knows our hearts just as intimately as God knew David's heart. Screen stories, in general, have been one of the ways God leads some of us outside of ourselves and our situations to look upon the things we are grappling with to find answers and understanding. Christian-based films as a possible

---

10. Brittanica.com Encyclopedia, "Parable."
11. Wilson, *Storytelling God*, 13.
12. Biblegateway.com Encyclopedia of the Bible, "Parable."
13. 2 Sam 12:1–7 (NRSVUE).
14. Wilson, *Storytelling God*, 125.

spiritual discipline place us in the position to have the modern-day David and Nathan experience to hear and see what we would typically not identify in our own lives under direct scrutiny.

To better understand story and storytelling, we would do our best to learn from the Divine Storyteller and be inspired to reach people's hearts for spiritual formation and transformation. How do we model after our Great Teacher, Jesus Christ, in becoming impactful and transformative storytellers? More specifically, how has film patterned the methods Jesus used as a storyteller? Christianity is a story recounting the life of Jesus Christ, his teachings, and the script detailing the way to discipleship.[15] Wilson took a closer look at Jesus' use of parables and revealed many things about God as a storyteller and God's thoughts towards us in his book *The Storytelling God*. Wilson introduces Jesus as a storyteller through his method of using parables. He lays a foundation by noting in Matthew 13:34 that Jesus does not speak to the people without using a parable, and he is fulfilling the Scripture of Psalm 78:2 in doing so.[16]

In reading the Scriptures, we can see that those who heard the parables of Jesus did not always discern their meaning. One example of a lack of discernment is when the disciples approached Jesus after he spoke to the crowds using parables and asked Jesus why he used the form of storytelling. In Matthew 13:10–17, Jesus explains to the disciples that only those who have been given insight into the mysteries of the kingdom of heaven will understand the stories he is telling. As we read further within the pericope, we understand that the intention behind using parables was to fulfill Scripture. "Jesus told the crowds all these things in parables; without a parable he told them nothing. This was to fulfill what had been spoken through the prophet: 'I will open my mouth to speak in parables; I will proclaim what has been hidden since the foundation.'"[17]

One of the issues that kept those listening to Jesus' parables from understanding was that their hearts resisted the spiritual revelations the messages conveyed. Crowds gathered to listen to Jesus, but many did not understand his words. The people laid eyes on Jesus and longed to be close to him, but they did not truly see who he was and what he was doing in their midst. Jesus explained how the people were not given spiritual insight into the meaning of the parables because their hearts were dull

---

15. Johnston, *Reel Spirituality*, 78.
16. Wilson, *Storytelling God*, 12.
17. Matt 13:34–35 (NRSVUE).

and unwilling to receive. However, those who had been given the gift of discernment would understand and be given more insight as a result. Jesus concludes by telling the disciples, "But blessed are your eyes, for they see, and your ears, for they hear."[18]

The passage in Matthew 13 makes it clear that Jesus was very aware that not everyone was going to understand or appreciate the moral of his stories. As I continue to argue for the efficacy of film as a tool in spiritually forming and guiding people, a necessary note must be established and reiterated: not everyone who watches a Christian-based film will discern, recognize, appreciate, or be transformed by the message (plot) or messengers (writers and filmmakers). We must approach viewing with discernment to engage a Christian-based film as a potential spiritual discipline (to support spiritual growth and deepen our relationship with Jesus Christ). We must come as viewers with humility, set aside preconceived biases and judgments, and surrender to the moving of the Holy Spirit within us to help discern the message intended for us as we openly engage to have ears that hear and eyes that see.

CINEMA: THE EVOLUTION OF STORYTELLING

As storytelling has evolved from the methods of Jesus to more visually creative and technical expressions, opportunities have opened up for The Gospel to be shared and for lives to be transformed by God's redemptive story. Considering the evolution of storying, I would develop an adapted description of parables concerning Christian-based films by saying: films can be parables that powerfully convey a message through a skillful rendering of "a familiar situation of common life."[19] Holly McClure, co-host of *Faith On Film*, describes films (Christian and faith-based) as the parables of today that God uses to reach those who usually do not go to church (much like we see Jesus using parables in the New Testament).[20] In her interview with T.C. Stallings about his role in the movie *Courageous*, Stallings shared his perspective on what discipleship should look like using faith-based screen stories. *Courageous* is a film produced by the Kendrick Brothers and Sherwood Films. Stallings, who has also appeared in other Christian films such as *War Room* and *A Question of Faith*, brings his perspective as

18. Matt 13:16 (NRSVUE).
19. Biblegateway.com Encyclopedia of the Bible, "Parable."
20. *Faith On Film #112*, T.C. Stallings Interview.

a Christian actor to the storytelling of these films. He emphasizes that we must tell the story of the Gospel in ways that stay true to the methods of Jesus and Scripture, ensuring we do not dilute the power of the message.[21]

A prime example of the method of parables in a film of today that holds to the display of God's love through others is found in the Lifetime television film, *Highway to Heaven* (2021). The movie is based on the television series created by Michael Landon bearing the same name. The television series *Highway to Heaven* was featured on the NBC network and ran from 1984–1989, starring Michael Landon as the angel Jonathan Smith. In 2021, the cable network, Lifetime, premiered the film adaptation of the television series.[22] The Christian themes that are present in the series address different life situations with a response of God's love shown through the angel. In the movie version, the angel Angela Stewart (Jill Scott) is sent by God to help at a school as a guidance counselor. In the work of fulfilling her assignment, she keeps beside her bed a reminder that says, "be the light that guides the way to someone's miracle." The film demonstrates the moral attitude by the example of Angela and those she influences to be a guiding light with intentionality and how God's love can shine through us.[23] But the question remains: How do we model storytelling as Jesus taught when examining films for the use of spiritual formation as a spiritual discipline? Faith leaders in particular must be equipped to intentionally integrate biblically-based movies and shows as a spiritual discipline to guide others in developing a relationship with Jesus Christ in their spiritual formation process.

The revelation of God was given to us in storytelling form, and parables were Jesus' method of choice in continuing the efficacy of storytelling to reach people's hearts.[24] Storytelling was not just a style preference for Jesus but also to fulfill the Scriptures. Beyond Jesus being a brilliant storyteller, Jesus is the story of God's love for humanity. "God chose to give the fullest revelation of Himself, not in a word but in a story. Jesus became the living story of who God is. God's primary source of self-revelation is story. God chooses to reveal Himself not as propositional truth but, rather, as experiential truth."[25] God knew the best way to reach our hearts was to tell us who our Creator was and to show us who our Lord is. More

21. *Faith On Film #112* (14:40—16:10).
22. Black, *Highway to Heaven*.
23. Black, *Highway to Heaven*.
24. Hall, "Jesus, God's Story," 10.
25. Hall, "Jesus, God's Story," 10.

importantly, God became "The Way" in the person of Jesus Christ. The scriptural reference that points to Jesus being God's revelation is found in John 14, as Jesus explains to the disciples that he is the way to the Father. Jesus tells them a story of comfort and a hopeful future, being prepared for those who believe in him.

As Thomas and Philip question Jesus about how to know the place and get there that Jesus storied, we experience a lack of discernment in their spiritual perspective. Jesus told them that he was the evidence—the story of proof—and if his Word was not enough, God's promised story he was living before them led the way. Jesus responds to Thomas, "I am the way and the truth and the life. No one comes to the Father except through me. If you know me, you will know my Father also. From now on you do know him and have seen him."[26]

However, Jesus' answer to the question was not enough to convince all of them to listen to the truth in the story Jesus was living. Philip had a follow-up question, and Jesus reiterated his story and provided additional information to drive home his point:

> Have I been with you all this time, Philip, and you still do not know me? Whoever has seen me has seen the Father. How can you say, 'Show us the Father'? Do you not believe that I am in the Father and the Father is in me? The words that I say to you I do not speak on my own, but the Father who dwells in me does his works. Believe me that I am in the Father and the Father is in me, but if you do not, then believe because of the works themselves.[27]

Jesus was telling the disciples and all who would revisit the account of the story that he was and is the visual story of God's existence and plan for humanity. Again, we can be reminded of Jesus' words that those with an ear will hear, and eyes will see (spiritually discerning) the meaning of the stories he told.

Jesus was aware of his disciples' and the crowd's lack of discernment. As the disciples followed him, they continued to misinterpret the story of God told through Jesus Christ and the invitation of reconciliation from God. Today, though we have much more foreknowledge of who Jesus was, what Jesus did, and God's plan of salvation through Jesus Christ, we still miss the opportunities when Jesus shows up in our lives, calling us into a closer relationship with him. Nonetheless, Wilson points out that parables have the

26. John 14:6–7 (NRSVUE).
27. John 14:9–11 (NRSVUE).

power to supernaturally transport us to the place they illustrate in the story: God's kingdom and will being done on earth and in heaven.[28] Encouraging spiritual imagination with discernment, Jesus showed his audiences a picture of God's character, will, and plan for humanity by using parables in hopes of seeing a point of view they would miss by thinking logically.

Wilson brings awareness to our capacity to often miss the mark of Jesus' intentions like the disciples did so many times. He bluntly conveys that the church has followed suit with Jesus' disciples being presumptuously clueless and often legalistic, like the Pharisees and Sadducees. We miss the mark in some of the following ways summarized based on Wilson's points: 1) the church thinks we know all the strategies of Jesus to save people, 2) we stifle people's spiritual growth much like the Pharisees with our dogma, 3) believe we are the experts in how to change people spiritually, and 4) so many times we move ahead of God as disciples without the Holy Spirit deterring our spiritual progress and hindering others as well.[29]

As mentioned in the previous chapter, we must move beyond the spiritual barriers that we have placed in the path of God, moving into the lives of others to be spiritually formed into the likeness of Christ. The traditional spiritual disciplines that Dallas Willard and Richard Foster outline fit the classification of a spiritual discipline with scriptural supporting evidence. I conclude that Christian-based screen stories can be classified as a spiritual discipline aligning with Willard and Foster's outlines and the evidence presented in this chapter of God's intention for storytelling to reach people's hearts imaginatively. God is story, created storytelling, and made us as storying human beings. Jesus is God's story in the flesh, and God is the Ultimate Storyteller. Elohim has created humanity with imaginations that can see creatively and the intelligent means to share visions with others in numerous ways, such as motion pictures. To say that dramatized stories on screen (Christian-based films or films, in general) cannot be a spiritual discipline is a conclusion that confines God and adds constraints to spiritual formation. Christian-based and faith-based screen stories are a means by which God is reaching, bonding, and transforming many people through the work of the Holy Spirit and bringing them into a deeper relationship with Jesus Christ—the expected results of practicing spiritual disciplines.

The support that the record of story gives concerning God's intention is undeniable according to Scripture and present in the parables, history,

---

28. Wilson, *Storytelling God*, 35.
29. Wilson, *Storytelling God*, 163.

education, technology, and entertainment. Films are the evolution of story, and God is still speaking through the genre of storytelling today for those who are willing to open themselves to the Holy Spirit to receive the discerning ear to hear and eye to see what the Spirit of God is saying to them.

THE SHACK: A CASE STUDY IN FAITH COMING TO LIFE WITH CONVICTION AND CONTROVERSY

The Shack (2017) is an example of how a movie brings to life the collaboration of Scripture, faith, and life lessons if we approach with the eyes to see and ears to hear. Examining the critical reception of this Christian-based film, offers insight into how Scripture can imaginatively inspire a screen story and the spiritual influence the screen story has had on spiritual and secular viewers.

The Shack is a story about a protagonist grappling with his relationship with God, himself, his family, his life, and his faith amidst tragedy, pain, grief, doubt, unforgiveness, and guilt. Viewers are introduced to the story of Mack Phillips (Sam Worthington), the protagonist, via narrator (Tim McGraw), his best friend, neighbor, and fellow church member. Within the film's first twenty minutes, we are given insight into Mack's past and present traumas contributing to his faith and relationship with God. As the story unfolds on screen, viewers travel with Mack on a journey with the Triune God that leads to healing and forgiveness. A liberation process by having an intimate encounter with the Triune God, addressing his past, facing his fears, and admitting his flaws delivers Mack from the layered weights of despair. In turn, he is renewed to see a hopeful future for himself and his family after significant loss and sadness.

The Shack was adapted from the #1 New York Times Best Sellers list novel, published in 2007 by William P. Young. There has been a great deal of controversy surrounding the film, reminiscent of the encounters Jesus had with the disciples and crowds who experienced his parables and challenges in finding their meaning. In the case of *The Shack*, the controversy mainly encompassed the "multiethnic and feminine portrayals of God."[30] Belinda Elliott, a contributing writer for the Christian Broadcasting Network (CBN. com), critically reviewed the book version preceding the film's production

---

30. Johnston, et al., *Deep Focus*, 40.

and release. She insightfully suggests a connection to Jesus' use of parables and how the film replicated the method to share the Gospel.[31]

There have been conflicting critiques concerning the theological messaging of *The Shack*. In addition to the previously mentioned controversy, many Christian communities have labeled the film as heretical because of the film's portrayal of the Trinity and biblical messaging.[32] Some secular movie critics conclude that the movie is oversentimental and too audaciously imagined for a Christian-based film.[33] Inclusively, the Christian and secular adverse critics of the film agree by only averaging to offer 1–2 stars in reviews. However, the story *The Shack* portrays has been widely received by the general Christian community. Since the reception of any story being told is subjective, the core idea insists on the need for discernment while engaging Christian screen stories as a spiritual discipline. The ability to discern the message the Holy Spirit is communicating to an individual or group in the spiritual formation process is critical to receive the possibilities of transformation in film as a spiritual discipline. Do we have the ears to hear and the eyes to see as Jesus continues to pose the question to believers watching screen stories, when we are constantly in a stance to criticize the source? I will explore more about the importance of preparing for film engagement for spiritual transformation in chapter 3.

Nonetheless, others have received *The Shack's* message with eyes to see and ears to hear what God is conveying to their lives personally. One of the actors in the movie, Country Music star Tim McGraw (Willie) describes *The Shack* as a potential "tool" for life sojourners searching for a spiritual connection, with themes of "love, compassion, and forgiveness."[34] McGraw recognized *The Shack* has the influential power to help people searching for understanding find some perspective in the story.

One crucial revelation that must be held onto if we engage film as a possible spiritual discipline is to approach viewing with openness and willingness to discern the Holy Spirit leading the process to receive the message of truth intended for us. Beyond sharing his testimony on the powerful influence of screen stories, Gareth Higgins suggests a prerequisite

---

31. Elliott, Review "What's So Bad," para 32.
32. Chandler, Review "'The Shack' film stirs debate," paras 3–4.
33. See Reviews Sobczynski, "The Shack"; Bradshaw, "The Shack Review"; and Gleiberman, "Film Review."
34. Law, Review "Tim McGraw Speaks Out," para 8.

of understanding the context of a film before viewing the movie.[35] Film theologians and scholars discussed in the next chapter offer similar advice about putting away preconceived conclusions about what a film portrays to receive the spiritual benefits that the movie may offer.

The use of storytelling to help people find meaning in their lives and work out life's complexities has been used since the beginning of time. *The Shack* has been a great conversation starter between many Christians and non-Christians with diverse perspectives. I have been a participant and have been privy to conversations surrounding themes in *The Shack* that are difficult to face. Some of those conversations have dealt with the loss of a child, why bad things happen to good people, and moving towards forgiving those who have hurt us. To harness the conversations around movies, Christlike leaders must cultivate intentionality in working with the film's influence on the psyche to spear spiritual growth. I am suggesting that Christian-based cinema has the potential to be among the spiritual disciplines that come alongside us as a tool (as parables are intended to do) with the power to bring spiritual clarity, nurture spiritual growth, and deepen our relationship with Jesus Christ. In the remainder of this chapter, I offer a degree of more detail on how and why film is a particularly powerful tool.

UNDERSTANDING THE PSYCHOLOGICAL IMPACT OF FILMS

In his discussion of Jesus' parables and storytelling as revelation, Kenley D. Hall notes stories' cognitive and emotional impact on human beings. Hall claims that neuroscience plays a part in the powerful dynamic storytelling has on someone. Drawing on the results of a recent brain-imaging study, Hall suggests that the human brain is "hardwired to respond to stories" and "our brains experience stories as if they were part of real life and as if they were happening to us."[36] The study concluded that our brains react to stories so intensely because "regions of the brain activated when an individual is processing the five 'traditional' senses (sight, sound, taste, smell, touch). The research discovered that these areas of the brain are activated when a person is engrossed in a story."[37]

---

35. Gareth Higgins, *How Movies Helped Saved My Soul*, 3.
36. See Day, "Use of Stories in Courses," 33–34.
37. See Day, "Use of Stories in Courses," 33–34.

As God created us to respond to physical stimuli when we are touched by a hug from a loving parent or the force of a falling object, human beings have also been created to be drawn in when the power of story touches our senses. How much more are our senses elevated when the stories we are visually exposed to pull us out of the logical spaces, we sometimes default to, and into the imaginations God gave us to see what we would otherwise not see? As noted in the Introduction, as a child Merritt could take a story he heard in church, that was shown to him through a movie and experience a loving pull towards Jesus Christ. The scenes of the crucifixion from the film were more than what he could imagine but an experience he could see, hear, feel, and understand. The screen story consumed him and activated a Holy Spirit enabled response within himself to lead him to a relationship with Jesus Christ.

Hall also makes the connection to the emotional impact stories have on human beings acknowledging the vantage point of former theology professor Jerome T. Walsh; saying that "a narrative appeals to more than just the intellect and makes its deepest impact at the level of emotion and the will."[38] "The emotional impact of the narrative comes from its ability to draw the reader or hearer into the story."[39] Films captivate and influence people to connect and discuss the plots of the stories. The power of storytelling can trigger emotions that will cause people to cry, get angry, yell at the screen, and leave the theater telling others how great or awful the film experience was to them. When our emotions are impacted by watching a movie, there is often always a response that is positive or negative. In spiritual formation, the Holy Spirit can influence how we acknowledge the emotions that are instigated as viewers and use the awareness to bring understanding and move us to a transformative response.

THE INTERSECTION OF PSYCHOLOGY AND SPIRITUALITY

Gareth Higgins offers insights into how films can contribute to our spirituality based on his personal experience and research. He concludes that "film should be treated with the same respect as church or poison, for it can change your life."[40] Arriving at his point, he acknowledges that film can

---

38. See Walsh, *Old Testament Narrative*, xii.
39. Hall, "Jesus, God's Story," 13.
40. Higgins, *How Movies Helped Saved My Soul*, xix.

Storytelling, Parables, and Christian-based Films'

"irritate and heal, challenge and affirm, inspire and sadden."[41] Although Higgins is speaking of movies in general and not isolating his vantage point to Christian-based films to find spirituality, as is the focus of the central argument, his claims support the consideration of incorporating Christian-based films as a possible spiritual discipline.

Merritt's experience at the movie theater shared in the introduction provides insight into how seeing a movie can lead to a transcendent and transformative encounter with the Holy Spirit. My experience watching the film, *Overcomer*, was similar to Merritt's. The Holy Spirit caused something in my brain to switch on to make a profound cognitive connection related to my life. As I was drawn deeper into the story, my emotions triggered a response that caused me to shed tears, raise my hands in the air, cheer for the protagonist, and leave believing I could overcome all the challenges I was facing at that time. Merritt's and my experiences were not just emotional but transformative moments that impacted how we would move forward in life. Stanley Hauerwas offers a possible explanation for the encounters that Merritt and I had, in which stories offer "the ability to step back and assess my own involvement in the adventure. They provide a standpoint that helps me see the limits and possibilities of my own role. Moral growth comes exactly through the testing of my role amid the other possibilities in the adventure."[42]

Film as a spiritual discipline is proposed to cause the same response. How powerful is it to bring people into an encounter with God and lead them to spiritual transformation by witnessing someone acting out a role on screen that is relatively relatable to their lives? When we are being brought into awareness and stretched to change by watching characters in a similar situation as we are dealing with in our lives can bring us insight. Movies can be a way the Holy Spirit guides us by addressing critical decisions that we grapple with daily. Moreso, a way to discipline us as we deal with the consequences of decisions that we have avoided. Walsh's insights into the decision-making process after being drawn into a story are highlighted by Hall: "A narrative compels us to make decisions as it unfolds. 'We are moved to accept or reject the values we perceive at work in the stories and to make moral judgments about characters and their deeds.'[43] These responses allow us to make sense of the story as it unfolds and ultimately determine whether

---

41. Higgins, *How Movies Helped Saved My Soul*, xix.
42. Berkman and Cartwright, *Hauerwas Reader*, 250.
43. See Walsh, *Old Testament Narrative*, xii.

or not we embrace the claims about life that the story makes."[44] As we observe the fields of neuroscience and literary intellectuals, Christian-based films as a possible spiritual discipline have the power to help us make transformative decisions. In fact, screen stories have spiritually formed many people without the church intentionally utilizing the genre as a spiritual tool for years. The reasons for the oversight of screen stories as a spiritual tool are further explored in the next chapter; however, the complicated history between the church and Hollywood is one of them. Nonetheless, knowing how human beings respond to stories equips faith leaders to use the information to support those entrusted to their care. Indeed, people are increasingly becoming aware of how movies recapture the meaning and power of the Gospel by bringing the stories to life on the screen.[45]

In their book *Positive Psychology at the Movies*, psychologists Ryan M. Niemiec and Danny Wedding introduce psychology's interrelation to film. Although their work is geared more towards how films contribute to positive psychology, well-being, and character building, there are three areas observed to be comprehensive to films as a possible spiritual discipline because the results are relative to holistic development. Their work provides insight into how we psychologically engage in a movie and how screen stories have the power to influence our thoughts and our responses to the film's themes: "The medium of film, more than any other art form, is able to portray the subtleties of the human mind—thoughts, emotions, instincts, and motives—and the mind's impact on behavior."[46] When considering how Christian-based films are viewed, understanding how they portray the Triune God, our faith, and how we engage humanity, we may comprehend the same notion of how we are being formed and are influenced to live out our faith.

According to Niemiec and Wedding, film is a universal language; "movies transcend all barriers and differences, whether these barriers are culture, language, religion, geographic borders, or belief systems."[47] Seeing film as a universal communication is vital to understanding the power film has to reach beyond the barriers to reach people in ways we often miss through other means of interaction. If film is universal in communicating to everyone, no matter where we come from, what we believe, how old

---

44. Hall, "Jesus, God's Story," 13.
45. Johnston, *Reel Spirituality*, 79.
46. Hall, "Jesus, God's Story," 13.
47. Niemiec and Wedding, *Positive Psychology*, 3.

we are, or how we identify, then the language of faith is not absent from the category of universality. Moreso, screen stories have the capacity to clarify messages that are often lost in translation through reading the Bible, hearing a sermon, or a Sunday School lesson unaccompanied by applicable interpretation.

Films communicate in a way that calls all human senses into a collaboration to get the point across. Niemiec and Wedding continue to lay the foundation for cinema as a universal language by saying, "Language is a way of communicating thoughts and feelings, and it is a system that has particular rules, signs, and symbols that shape it and make it meaningful. Similar rules are found in movies; however, cinema is not restricted to one country or group of people. Therefore, movies are a commentary on more than society—they inform us about the human condition."[48] I would also say that films can be a way that God communicates to humanity about who God is, our understanding of how we view God, how we see ourselves in the world God created, and they can be a means to wrestle with what we believe is true about God. Films can be vessels informing us about our faith's vital signs and how we live our faith in the world—whole, wounded, lost, or as a beacon of light.

In considering the psychology of films and how they communicate to viewers to inform us about what we internally and externally understand about God, ourselves, and the world around us, Niemiec and Wedding introduce three layers that shape a viewer's experience: plot, subtext, and character.[49] The plot is the infrastructure and support given to the subtext, while the subtext provides a more profound meaning that evokes viewers as the narrative builds.[50] Within the subtext of a film are found levels of communication in the psychological landscape of the characters, culture and customs of the setting location, and social and political dynamics of communities and organizations.[51] Also, the subtext portrays metaphors that accentuate the film's themes through the collaboration of cinematography, lighting, sound, set design, and special effects.[52] Also, music has a role in

---

48. Niemiec and Wedding, *Positive Psychology*, 3.
49. Niemiec and Wedding, *Positive Psychology*, 3–5.
50. Niemiec and Wedding, *Positive Psychology*, 3.
51. Niemiec and Wedding, *Positive Psychology*, 3.
52. Niemiec and Wedding, *Positive Psychology*, 3.

Discerning Beyond the Screen

the subtext leading viewers to empathize with a character or influencing their judgments about a character by what they hear.[53]

Exploring more character communication, Niemiec and Wedding share that the structure of a character is built upon corporeality, psyche, and sociality: "referring to the character's outer appearance, their inner state, and traits, and their social interactions, roles, and environmental interaction, respectively" are essential for identifying the character's strengths.[54] Niemiec and Wedding acknowledge the creativity of filmmakers who can use images, sound, and evocative power of film to explore characters' minds, identities, and internal worlds.[55] The layers of the plot, subtext, and characters in a movie all play a role in influencing viewers, but viewers play a more significant role by creating meaning or interpreting the screen story for their lives.[56] Niemiec and Wedding categorize positive psychology movies as films that align in seeking to integrate the good and bad that we experience in life, which is the fullness of the human experience. The focus is to emphasize well-being and character strengths.[57] Viewers are influenced in various ways by a movie that either pulls them in or repels them from the message being communicated. There are many reasons why either may occur based on the psychological impacts the film is having on the viewer. Niemiec and Wedding mention Walt Disney's process of creating films, understanding that their success in communicating to viewers was not based on age but on the inner thoughts within everyone (the "unspoiled spot") that we need to help them remember.[58] They expand upon Disney's ideology in connection to positive psychology movies in that these movies "speak to that unspoiled spot that is present in all of us; when it is tapped, cinematic elevation and cinematic admiration unfold, leading viewers to take action that improves both their living and the lives of others."[59]

Just as Disney, Niemiec, and Wedding have understood that there are experiences, emotions, and untapped thoughts within us that have yet to be discovered or need support in reigniting significance to our lives, the same has undergirded the claim for my central argument. Engaging film as a

---

53. Niemiec and Wedding, *Positive Psychology*, 3.
54. Niemiec and Wedding, *Positive Psychology*, 4; 7.
55. Niemiec and Wedding, *Positive Psychology*, 14.
56. Niemiec and Wedding, *Positive Psychology*, 4.
57. Niemiec and Wedding, *Positive Psychology*, 7, 20.
58. Niemiec and Wedding, *Positive Psychology*, 20.
59. Niemiec and Wedding, *Positive Psychology*, 7, 20.

spiritual discipline with an understanding of the psychological triggers will lead to either the spiritual formation process or a rejection of how the movie may nurture or hinder a relationship with Jesus Christ. Christian-based films being considered and utilized as a spiritual discipline to support spiritual growth and deepen our relationship with Jesus Christ has the power to reach the "unspoiled spot" that Disney identified as intergenerational and what Niemiec and Wedding introduced as transcending barriers. The place they speak of is what I describe as the humanistic longing to seek and find God and meaning in the world we live in. A film's power to help discover the two is God's gift to those who dare to traverse the cinematic world.

To conclude this chapter, many may agree that films, like any genre of art, are subject to individual interpretations. Recognizing the idiosyncrasies individuals have when viewing a movie based on their psychological and spiritual influences, can offer an understanding of how they may be open to being spiritually formed by the cinematic experience. As faith leaders, we are responsible for being aware of contributing factors to the spiritual development of those entrusted to our care so that we may come alongside them with affirmation or clarification. We are analytical beings and can be extremely critical regarding spirituality, as we often deal with life and death surrounding our faith and belief systems. However, completely disregarding God's ability to reach people's hearts and transform their lives in ways we think are not valid is an arrogant mistake. As Johnston reminds us, "Movies are a window through which God speaks."[60] And God speaks to us through stories that are brought to life in images and sound that have a unique capacity to prompt a response within us. Recognizing that storytelling is a powerful influence has been essential for the movie industry.[61] Christian leaders also acknowledging the influence of films, by using screen stories as a spiritual discipline, can be transformational for the church.

No matter how elaborate the story is being told or poorly illustrated, Jesus has the power to reach whomever and however he chooses. Romans 8:28 is a great starting place before we begin to judge what God will and will not use to bring glory to the Lord and work for the good of those who belong and have a purpose in God.[62] Wilson highlights the heart of Jesus in this way: "Here is a sweet glimpse into Jesus' pastoral heart. And it is a revelation of two senses of his ministry in relation to the disciples. 'As they

60. Johnston, *Reel Spirituality*, 161–62.
61. Johnston, *Reel Spirituality*, 100.
62. Rom 8:28 (NRSVUE).

were able to hear it' shows us that they were able to hear it. It also shows us that Jesus spoke when they were able to hear it. The Word gave them ears to hear the word."[63] Wilson is referencing Mark 4:33–34, when Jesus spoke only in parables and then privately explained the meaning of the parables to the disciples. Screen stories may be the very way Jesus knows that some will hear him when he speaks to them about who God is and what Jesus has done for them. The transformative work and spiritual formation that comes from the encounter is the work of the Holy Spirit, not ours. As faith leaders, we have a responsibility to be equipped with discerning and pastoral hearts to meet with them after the screen story has been told, the Holy Spirit speaks, and the lights come on to journey alongside them as spiritual nurturers.

---

63. Wilson, *Storytelling God*, 171.

Chapter Three

Establishment and Flourishing of Cinema's Influence and Responses

ROBERT K. JOHNSTON, PROFESSOR and theologian of film and culture, says that "what many churches have forgotten and preachers ignore, the movie theater recognizes: 'story reigns supreme.'"[1] In expanding on the power of storytelling as it relates to film, Johnston's collaborative work with his colleagues from Fuller Theological Seminary, Craig Detweiler, and Kutter Callaway express that churches have had diverse responses to the increasingly available media projects.[2] As films are being made readily accessible not just by going to the movie theater but by the click of a button on a streaming device or by a voice command connected to a smart television, more people have the opportunity to engage in screen stories. Furthermore, "movies serve not simply as a commodity but as the primary storytelling medium of the twenty-first century, interpreting reality for us, providing us with a common language, and acting as a type of cultural glue."[3]

Even though some Christians still advocate for visual media abstinence or at least restrictive engagement, several others are jumping into the rushing media wave with both feet. Johnston, Detweiler, and Callaway say that "a larger and increasing number of Christians have recognized that

---

1. Johnston, *Reel Spirituality*, 100.
2. Johnston, et al., *Deep Focus*, 34.
3. Johnston, et al., *Deep Focus*, 10.

since the church's core message is a story, and since movies are our culture's primary storytelling medium, dialogue, and interaction are a better response."[4] Another response Christians can consider resulting from the core idea is the storytelling of Christian-based films as a possible spiritual discipline. The targeted reaction is both conversational and interactive in hopes of experiencing one, if not all, of these: spiritual revelation, transcendence, formation, and transformation. Several film and culture theologians highly suggest Christians watch a movie openly and leave preconceived ideas, doctrine, theology, and prejudices at the door. The same practice is necessary to use Christian-based films as a possible spiritual discipline. Johnston conveys five Theologian/Critic approaches to viewing films that he says are the primary responses of the Church: avoidance, caution, dialogue, appropriation, and divine encounter.[5]

Avoidance is concretely a response of boycotting movies.[6] Caution is an awareness of a film's influence and causes for discrimination in viewing movies.[7] Dialogue is an open two-way conversational engagement between film and theology.[8] Examining Johnston's approaches, in light of spiritual formation, are insightful as a viewer's attention increases with films potentially leading to transcendence and transformation. Considering appropriation, Johnston says, "those who seek to appropriate a movie's vision of life recognize that movies can offer insight to the Christian viewer about the nature of the human. There is something new that a movie can provide a Christian. More than dialogue is called for. The theologian must be receptive to encountering spirit in a new guise and only then turn to respond from the viewer's own theological point of view."[9] And last but not least, a divine encounter is "a sacramental capacity to provide the viewer an experience of transcendence."[10]

I agree with Johnston that a Christian's better response to movies is dialogue and interaction. He also says that we first must be open to viewing a film on "its own terms."[11] The viewer must also have an open mind, heart,

---

4. Johnston, et al., *Deep Focus*, 34.
5. Johnston, *Reel Spirituality*, 41–58.
6. Johnston, *Reel Spirituality*, 43–45.
7. Johnston, *Reel Spirituality*, 45–49.
8. Johnston, *Reel Spirituality*, 49–54.
9. Johnston, *Reel Spirituality*, 54–56.
10. Johnston, *Reel Spirituality*, 57–58.
11. Johnston, *Reel Spirituality*, 49.

spirit, and soul to every entity that makes a movie powerful and influential in its construct. In the case of spiritual formation, the Holy Spirit is the necessary Presence to have a transformative dialogue and a Divine interaction. I will dedicate time in this chapter to indirectly weaving together Johnston, Detweiler, and Callaway's approaches and other film scholars' insights to provide pillars of support in recognizing film and cinema's relationship with the church, theology, spirituality, and culture.

A BRIEF HISTORY OF AMERICAN CINEMA'S EVOLVING RELATIONSHIP WITH THE CHURCH

While I continue to establish the consideration of Christian-based films as a possible spiritual discipline, knowing cinema's historical connection to the church is critical in understanding how movies have been a means of spiritual growth and discipleship in its early development.[12] Film and culture theologians have accomplished work embodying the Catholic's belief in sacramental imagination. The results of their work contribute to understanding divine encounters and highlight God's revelatory grace toward humanity in movies.[13] Initially, films produced in the early 1900s were silent, relying on action and animation for entertainment. However, the desire for storytelling pushed the art form beyond visual acrobatics, motivating filmmakers to create plots with meaningful stories.[14] As moving pictures evolved in the early 1900s, the use of storytelling in the medium increased.[15] In the connection of film to the church, many early religious movies were made by evangelists in the early 1900s. Johnston details that filmmakers began to expose the storytelling presented in the theater and captured the artistry on film. The transition from silent film to theatrical cinema opened the door to sharing plays with religious themes and the portrayal of biblical stories.[16] Among the first of the church and the evangelists to utilize movies as a tool for discipleship was Herbert Booth, son

---

12. Johnston provides historical insight into film's inception in *Reel Spirituality*. Knowing the history of cinema will add appreciation to the evolution of the genre, and Johnston's book provides ample information.
13. Johnston, et al., *Deep Focus,* 124.
14. Stoddart, "The Circus and Early Cinema," 6.
15. Stoddart, "The Circus and Early Cinema," 6.
16. Johnson, *Reel Spirituality*, 31–32.

of William and Catherine Booth, the founders of The Salvation Army.[17] Herbert Booth recognized the power of film to interest people in coming to Sunday lectures and prayer meetings, where he showed clips of hymns, prayers, and sermons through short films with the help of cinematographer Joseph Perry.[18] The diversity of film themes was present in the initial growth. Still, the genre's attraction within the church was to portray the morals, values, and reverence of religious life through cinema's storytelling method, as the churches were even used as movie theaters.[19]

Despite several decades were the American church boycotted the industry in the one hundred years since Booth and Perry, the church has recently become more involved in filmmaking. In *Cinema as Pulpit*, Ryan Parker references that the Protestant ministers have discerned God's presence in films and have seen opportunities to evangelize through the genre. Some clergy began making their own Christian-based films and incorporating movie viewings within their strategic ministry plans.[20] Christians began to pick up where Henry Booth left off and saw cinema as a way to bring people into the mission of discipleship. For instance, The Kendrick Brothers and Sherwood Pictures in Albany, Georgia, are Christian film producers who discerned God's move in making films and established their production company in 2003. Their first movie was a low-budget feature-length film, *Flywheel* (2003), followed by *Facing the Giants* (2006).[21]

Alex and Stephen Kendrick were informed by reading a survey that film was increasingly becoming more of an influence in culture than the church.[22] Since 2003, they have produced more movies accompanied by books and curricula to support spiritual growth.[23] The Kendrick Brothers and Sherwood Pictures are not the only Christians, pastors, and churches that have discerned God's presence in film and redeemed the genre for ministry. However, they are examples of those who have succeeded in using movies to disciple and provide sources to consider in supporting my claim of utilizing Christian-based film as a prospective spiritual discipline.

17. Johnson, *Reel Spirituality*, 32.
18. Johnson, *Reel Spirituality*, 32.
19. Johnson, *Reel Spirituality*, 32.
20. Parker, *Cinema as Pulpit*, 6.
21. Kendrick, *Flywheel* and *Facing the Giants*.
22. Parker, *Cinema as Pulpit*, 7.
23. Kendrick Brothers, "Our Projects."

THEOLOGICAL INSIGHTS AND CONTROVERSIES OF CHRISTIAN-BASED FILMS

The church must acknowledge and prepare for the fact that conversations about God happen daily outside the four walls of ecclesial buildings and ministry organizations without their influence or consideration.[24] One of the most popular cultural gatherings inviting theological conversations is watching and discussing movies. Johnston says, "for movies seek to engage us, their viewers, as whole human beings. They invite—we might almost say, demand—our response. And it is easily given."[25] He adds, "after seeing a film, we go with friends to Starbucks or a restaurant to have a cup of coffee and to talk about whether we liked the film or not. We want to share our reactions and responses."[26] Movies spark conversations that many sermons, Bible studies, and Sunday School lessons may not. I have witnessed several people resist going to church but willingly engage in a discussion about God after watching a movie over a meal. Instead of becoming discouraged about what is not happening within the confines of the church, Christians need to discern, as Johnston states, "how God might be using film to reveal something of the divine to us."[27] When considering Christian-based films as a potential spiritual discipline, film theology is crucial to establishing a structure to introduce a framework for the practice. We must acknowledge the preconceived theologies that we bring to our engagement and interpretation of films. Johnston, Detweiler, and Callaway offer greater insight into how we approach a film with our theological biases:

> Each comes to film from a defined theological perspective and thus finds a one-sided imbalance between Hollywood and the church, between movies and theology. For the most part, they believe that movies are too often in the business of theological subversion (though how "subversion" would be defined differs greatly). Thus, they advise caution for the religious viewer.[28]

They advise and caution on preparing to view a film with a theological intention by saying:

---

24. Johnston, *Reel Spirituality*, 14.
25. Johnston, *Reel Spirituality*, 14.
26. Johnston, *Reel Spirituality*, 14.
27. Johnston, *Reel Spirituality*, 14.
28. Johnston, et al., *Deep Focus*, 119.

But to typically begin one's interaction with a movie by first staking out one's theological and/or ethical position before experiencing the story on its own terms risks both theological imperialism and faulty artistic judgments.[29]

In weighing the previous film theologians' insights, introspection allows us to sift through and, potentially, weed out preconceived theological biases that may discredit a film's intentions. We must acknowledge and address our theological positioning before approaching Christian-based movies as a prospective spiritual discipline to support spiritual growth and deepen our relationship with Jesus Christ. I emphasize again that the intentional surrender to the work of the Holy Spirit is critical if we spiritually embrace dialogue with a Christian-based film that leads to a divine encounter, resulting in spiritual formation. A posture of surrender to the Holy Spirit is necessary because we often come to a movie full of ourselves.[30] When we bring too much of what we think, believe, and expect to the movie with subtle or advert resistance, we may walk away from the film with a bitter taste or no appetite to encounter viewing with spiritual intention again. As for the church, the worst scenario that I envision when we place more of ourselves in the process rather than yielding to the move of the Holy Spirit is becoming a stumbling block; hindering the spiritual transformation of those who may have a divine encounter watching any movie. Johnston, Detweiler, and Callaway express similar concerns observing the church's struggle to move outside of itself as an influential organism:

> And the church's seeming inability to cultivate these kinds of generative spaces has led to an increasingly fragmented and tribalized notion of Christian community—one comprising isolated echo chambers filled with people who cannot communicate, much less commune, with those who do not think, talk, and act exactly as they do. The question then is whether the church will simply continue to echo the wider culture and its politics or whether she will lead the way by modeling a more constructive form of public dialogue.[31]

Several times I have entered into dialogue with Christian colleagues about Christian-based films, and more times than not, a squint overshadows their faces. The subsequent response is often related to the questionable theological messaging many of the available films portray. Before

---

29. Johnston, et al., *Deep Focus*, 119.
30. Johnston, et al., *Deep Focus*, 119.
31. Johnston, et al., *Deep Focus*, 198–99.

moving forward in the conversation, the first question must be whether the movie is a Christian-based or faith-based film. Like most film and culture theologians, I have studied and observed God in every genre of film, careful to understand that the filmmakers do not classify or had no motive of making their movies faith-based. Noting the distinction is essential for the church as an institution and Christians as individuals if we consider utilizing Christian-based films as a viable spiritual tool for discipleship and formation. A more significant concern for theological messaging arises in furthering the dialogue with colleagues when focusing on Christian-based or faith-based films. Johnston's outlines of avoidance, caution, dialogue, appropriation, and divine encounter help assess messaging concerns.

Various critics are concerned with the theology portrayed in some Christian-based films.[32] However, the concerns should not warrant refraining from seizing the opportunity to have a significant dialogue about how Christian-based films may contribute to spiritual development. As Christians, being fully open to discerning how God may speak to us or someone seeking spiritual formation in a movie is a matter of accountability. Discerning possible experiences of transcendence or transformation led by the Holy Spirit through a Christian-based film is worth the consideration, time, and work to remove our preconceived judgments about a movie's theology to witness God working all things together for the good of spiritual formation.[33] The good for many could be the gift of salvation. Spiritual transformation is the potential good for many others who have come to know Jesus Christ as their Lord and Savior. The spiritual work that films have the capacity to accomplish outside of the constraints of a church's brick and mortar, as well as the doctrine of how a church functions, is to be acknowledged. In *Deep Focus*, the thought is expressed in this way: "For now, we acknowledge that movies provide for many alternate forms of transcendence—encounters that take place outside the confines of the church but are nonetheless understood to be religiously significant."[34]

Johnston provides six theological reasons why a Christian should initiate dialogue using film as he says, "movies can provide their viewers

---

32. The following examples of the critical responses to Christian films represent secular and Christian perspectives: Barber, "The Problem with Christian Films," and Chang, "A Christian critic wrestles."

33. Rom 8:28.

34. Johnston, et al., *Deep Focus*, 18.

both experiences of life and greater understanding of their culture."[35] I will briefly outline each theological reason and then highlight how the points support considering Christian-based films as a potential spiritual discipline.

Common grace and human culture make up the first reason on Johnston's list. He points out that in the book of Genesis, God blessed all creation. God looked upon all creation and called the finished work good. As Christians, we misconstrue the call to be set apart from the world and take the mandate to mean that God is not part of the world. When we look beyond our theological biases, we can set ourselves up to see God moving in the spaces and places we have not considered. Our biases position us in a spiritual silo that abstains from seeing the work of God, which is beyond our understanding.

Johnston says, "as Christian theology has rightly concentrated its understanding of humankind on our pervasive sin and consequent need of redemption, it has sometimes wrongly emptied human culture both of its actual achievement and of God's ongoing presence. Theology has too often failed to see that God is still at work throughout his creation."[36] Although Johnston is speaking of all films, I am focused on his reason for Christian-based film dialogue; to not throw the baby out with the bath water because we have an issue with the theology of a Christian-based film and write it off as blasphemous. Discussion can help identify the wheat growing with the weeds and serve as an example of how to identify flawed theology present in movies.[37]

"Spirit and spirit" is the second reason presented by Johnston, which emphasizes that the Spirit of God is still searching the hearts and seeking to connect the spirits of all humanity.[38] Johnston points out:

> If the Spirit is active in and through the human spirit, then the potential for the sacred is present across our human endeavor. Yet Christian theology continues largely to ignore the mundane, the ordinary experience of human life.[39]

As Johnston elaborates on the Spirit's action, his reason for engagement concerning the role of the Holy Spirit is where I reiterate the

---

35. Johnston, et al., *Deep Focus*, 64–72.
36. Johnston, *Reel Spirituality*, 66–67.
37. In Matt 13:24–30, Jesus tells the parable of weeds among the wheat.
38. Johnston, *Reel Spirituality*, 67.
39. Johnston, *Reel Spirituality*, 69.

essential acknowledgment of the Holy Spirit's work within film being a spiritual discipline.

> In some circles there has been an unfortunate narrowing of the Spirit's role to the Christian community and a limitation of the Spirit's relation with our spirit to the extraordinary. The result of this constriction of the Holy Spirit's role has been denial of the human spirit.[40]

To say that the Holy Spirit cannot actively work in a person's life through films is a misleading narrative. Also, without the Holy Spirit, spiritual formation and transformation cannot be fruitful in the spiritual practice of Christian-based movies as a viable spiritual discipline.

Johnston's third reason for dialogue, hearing God through non-Christians, is not my primary focus for the core idea since I am evaluating the genre as a potential spiritual discipline. However, Johnston's central point is that God can use all things that are truth and untruth.[41] To place constraints on who God is and how God works is to forget that theology is our process of seeking to know God, not putting a definitive label on our Creator. An example of the constraints we place on God is found in John 4, where Jesus encounters the woman at the well. He tells her that we must come to God in Spirit and in Truth, illustrating how people can be set free from a lack of understanding.[42]

Johnston suggests, "if viewers will join in community with a film's storyteller, letting the movie's images speak with their full integrity, they might be surprised to discover that they are hearing God as well."[43] For Christians representing the church, we must remain ever mindful that God cannot and will not be placed in the confined boxes many of us tend to put the omnipresent, omniscient, and omnipresent Spirit into with our theology. Bringing our superior theology to a non-Christian or Christian-based film will place us in a situation to see more of what we are presupposed to see rather than seeing the revelation God is showing us in Spirit and Truth. When we place our theology aside, viewing Christian-based films as a possible spiritual discipline will require humility that engages and embraces a film's "full integrity." Our surrender positions us to have eyes to see and ears

---

40. Johnston, *Reel Spirituality*, 69–70.
41. Johnston, *Reel Spirituality*, 72.
42. John 4:5–30.
43. Johnston, *Reel Spirituality*, 72.

to hear what the Spirit of the Lord is saying to draw us closer to Jesus Christ and nurture our spiritual development.

The following three reasons address films' images, narratives, and characters. The orchestration of all three to challenge our theology and position our spirits to receive God's message is critical in communicating to viewers. The first among the most important points to consider is that God is the "Image-maker" and has created us to be "image-makers," giving image-makers the ability to transport viewers to an experience of joy.[44] Johnston conveys that Protestants need to reevaluate the theology of images for "image's ability to transport the viewer to some more central place, to provide the viewer that experience of 'Joy' . . ."[45]

The second reason is in addressing the theology's narrative shape, Johnston discusses the role of storytelling that I have discussed in chapter 2. He points out storytelling is at the root of Christian theology as a testimony of what has been seen and lived, and "the church has forgotten that the heart of its theology is story."[46] With that being said, theologians' acknowledgment of storytelling's significance has often been disregarded. Johnston expresses the importance of story in the perspective of theology by saying:

> Stories are performative; they give meaning to facts. In the process they help answer questions concerning who we are and point us to that larger truth which lies beyond our grasp. But what has this to do with theology and film? A growing number of persons are finding that movies as story provide their viewers a means of recapturing the meaning and power of our story-shaped gospel, something we have all too often abstracted.[47]

Films have the power to place people before us and tell their stories that we can relate to through shared, similar, or contrasting experiences.

Theology's dialogical character is the final reason listed by Johnston. He says, "the world (culture) must be seen as theology's setting (it is the form in which we think and learn) and application (theology rethinks God's thoughts in every generation)."[48] Johnston follows up by saying, "personal experience matters theologically. Varied experiences, for example, sometimes cause women to read Scripture differently than men . . . what

---

44. Johnston, *Reel Spirituality*, 76–78.
45. Johnston, *Reel Spirituality*, 76–78.
46. Johnston, *Reel Spirituality*, 78–80.
47. Johnston, *Reel Spirituality*, 78–80.
48. Johnston, *Reel Spirituality*, 83.

is thought reasonable also varies culturally."[49] His statement that theological experiences matter can align with biblical reconciliation leader Brenda Salter McNeil's "theology matters" sentiments.[50]

As today's generations engage in movies' images, narratives, and characters that harmonize before our very eyes on a screen, our imaginations transport to a tangible view that causes us to rethink and respond to possibilities. The filmmakers' creative direction and cinematography techniques, artistic production sets, costume designs, sights, sounds, music, acting, capturing of culture transcending time and space, and final editing transport us to the places we only dream possible. The images we see on the screens bring to life many ideas we would otherwise not consider possible.[51] The narratives storied throughout a movie employ a plot that often reaches a place of empathy, conviction, rage, healing, and a plethora of emotions that cause a response beyond our pleasure or distaste. The characters become us, and we become the characters. We witness how the story impacts their lives and relates to our own lives, even more so, how the characters convince us to take a closer look at ourselves and the world around us, resulting in dialogue, appropriation, or a divine experience. All of these forms of imagination realized in films are powerful for the use of spiritual formation. As Johnston et al conclude, "Movies have, at times, a sacramental capacity to provide the viewer an experience of transcendence."[52] Transcendence and transformation are the manifested power elements that Christian-based films, as a viable spiritual discipline, have to provide for those who engage in spiritual formation.

The reasons and insights that Johnston and other theologians offer provide a theological basis to take on the posture of openness for my central argument claim. Engaging Christian-based film as a potential spiritual discipline to ultimately have a divine encounter that leads to spiritual growth and a closer relationship with Jesus Christ is a viable option for numerous people when used with discernment and intentionality. I expand and take Johnston's thought a step further in saying that Christian-based films can be tools for spiritual growth in a culture increasingly moving away from the church as a source of spiritual sustenance.

---

49. Johnston, *Reel Spirituality*, 83.
50. Johnston, *Reel Spirituality*, 83.
51. Johnston, et al., *Deep Focus*, 67–88.
52. Johnston, et al., *Deep Focus*, 123.

COMMUNICATING AND INFLUENCING SPIRITUAL DEVELOPMENT THROUGH CINEMA

The pioneer of the self-improvement genre, Dale Carnegie, shares in his 1937 book, *How to Win Friends and Influence People*, that "dramatizing your ideas" is a significant way to influence people.[53] Dramatization is at the heart of storytelling and attraction to the cinema. Carnegie provides several techniques to win people over, but his acknowledgment of the method of influence that movies and television have on people is the use of drama. His sentiment is that if drama works for the visual media to influence people, why not use drama to reach people in every aspect of life? Again, the theory that drama or storytelling influences people is not a new concept. Reiterating Jesus' use of storytelling is a reminder of the method of efficacy he used to reach his audience. Movies are at our disposal as a method of dramatization to present the message of faith and formation that communicates beliefs that may get lost in translation through a sermon, study, or ordinary conversation. For many people, the adage "seeing is believing" is fitting for films' influence on spiritually developing individuals. Carl Plantinga, Professor of Film, says, "stories presented on screens have the potential to influence individuals and cultures because they are pervasive, because they are stories (in narrative form), and because they partake of the special capacities of audiovisual media."[54] An example of a movie communicating and influencing a transformative response was witnessed by viewing a non-Christian-based film, *Hunger Games*. CBS *This Morning* aired a story on the power of influence cinema has had on society during the unrest in Myanmar in 2021. Protestors in Myanmar have taken the three-finger symbol seen in the popular culture film *Hunger Games* (2012) and adopted the symbol as their own sign of protest.[55] The CBS report is an example of how movies have a psychological impact on human beings and our society, with the power to influence a transformative response. Plantinga also provides additional insight into how the *Hunger Games* has influenced culture based on moral and ideological judgment.[56]

As previously noted, the power of movies has been of great theological, ethical, and moral concern for how they may negatively influence viewers

---

53. Carnegie, *How to Win Friends*, 181–85.
54. Plantinga, "The Power of Screen Stories," 1.
55. Mason, "Powerful Salute."
56. Plantinga, "Moralities and Characters," 6.

to emulate certain spiritual, psychological, and cultural behaviors or trends. For the same reason that some have avoided or cautioned against watching films, others have seen the benefits of how films effectively communicate. Also, recognizing how movies have been influential in educating viewers on positive behaviors that can help them process their thoughts and emotions. The idea is that films unexpectedly engage our senses in a way that reaches beyond the emotional, spiritual, psychological, and cultural barriers that we have in place. Plantinga notes David Brooks' idea that screen stories are educators that sneak in through the back door and communicate persuasively to our emotions.[57] I am suggesting that spiritual discipline be intentionally placed at our emotional back doors to seize the opportunity for a divine encounter that leads to spiritual growth and transformation.

The primary influential messages Christian-based films should communicate are the lessons, principles, and practices of Jesus Christ. If the film does not connect to Jesus Christ and align with his teachings, the film is not Christian-based, in my observation. Faith-based and inspirational films may have a spiritual influence that encourages, inspires, or motivates people through the stories being shared. However, if Jesus Christ and what he taught are not included or the center points of focus, the films are not Christian-based.

There are various responses that movies may cause viewers to have. When considering how a person is processing the inward and outward spiritual experiences they have daily, films have the audio, visual, and imaginative power to sort through various emotions, questions, and scenarios that are often difficult to do in a linear state of contemplation in one's mind. As a probable spiritual discipline, Christian-based movies can provide a method of influence to engage all the senses to have a divine encounter that leads to transcendence and spiritual formation. Viewers may process the message the films are communicating with responses of salvation, growing as a disciple of Christ, and engaging in the world as followers of Christ with efficacy.

Spiritual formation is possible in a viewer watching a Christian-based film when the storytelling being dramatized on the screen before them influences a response of retrospection, introspection, and consideration that leads to spiritual growth or a deeper relationship with Jesus Christ. Setting the framework to watch a Christian-based film as a probable spiritual discipline, the viewer becomes trained to watch screen stories with the same potential reactions. However, viewers intentionally

---

57. Plantinga, "The Rhetoric of Screen Stories," 19–20.

align their responses to nurture their spiritual growth, understanding, and relationship with Jesus Christ.

Movies have the power to trigger a memory of the past, make us think about how to manage a current situation, or empathize with how others experience life differently from our own. The objective is to nurture an environment with training for a viewer to possibly have a salvific experience like James Merritt while watching Jesus being crucified on a movie screen. Another possibility is like myself, relating to Hannah (Arin Thompson) being encouraged as she ran a difficult race in *Overcomer,* strengthened to believe that I too would overcome my own challenges after watching the film. In both Merritt's and my cases, seeing was believing and influenced us to deepen our relationship with Jesus Christ and grow spiritually as disciples.

CHRISTIAN-BASED FILMS AS A WAY TO DISCIPLE POP CULTURE GENERATIONS

Robert K. Johnston re-tells a story by Bishop Willimon about growing up in Greenville, South Carolina. As a young disciple attending a Sunday service, Willimon slipped out the church's back door with his buddies to go to the movie theater.[58] Telling Willimon's story emphasized how films have been a powerful force in our culture across generations. Movies have influenced people within and outside of the church walls. Knowing that movies have the power to lure young people away from church, how do we redeem such influence? Christians have a mandate of discipleship, which is essential to make disciples of all nations (cultures).[59] The church has to consider the best ways to reach popular culture in the face of church decline and increased media engagement. Already dealing with a discipleship dilemma, the church's isolation due to a global pandemic in 2020 added pressures unfamiliar to the entire world for the churched and unchurched in pop culture. Discipling young Christians by being aware of what they are consuming through various media sources allows for opportunities to learn about their struggles and hold ourselves accountable as spiritual leaders. Hauerwas and Willimon bring to light that Jesus calls us to be like salt as disciples. Jesus teaches the disciples about being salt in respect to enhancing the world by spreading the truth of the Gospel and all the lessons he has taught for the sake of making more disciples. For Hauerwas

---

58. Johnston, *Reel Spirituality,* 22.
59. Matt 28:19.

and Willimon, we must measure our witnessing salt so we are not causing people's sickness.[60] Moreover, the young people I have mentored and ministered to have expressed how judgmental, self-righteous, closed-minded, and unloving multi-generational Christians have been in their lives, which can fall under too much salt.

Being mindful of the preparations and strategies necessary that Hauerwas and Willimon categorize as having the right balance of salt to influence pop culture is a critical evaluation the church must consistently make. Engaging and evaluating Christian-based films as a possible spiritual discipline to support young Christians' (and all generations') spiritual growth and deepen their relationship with Jesus Christ is finding salt balance. Utilizing Christian-based films as a tool in spiritual formation supports Hauerwas and Willimon's claim that the church needs to be the right amount of salt related to helping young Christians survive in the world. The generations we are discipling today need strategic equipping for their real fight as believers, which Ephesians 6:10–19 informs us of in spiritual warfare. The battlegrounds within social media and streaming sources often influence a response with negative results. That said, young Christians have to survive as a Christian in the world, with few Christians in their support circles that reinforce and build a Christian community. We must solidify ways to strengthen pop culture in Christ. The cultural shift adds a different dimension to the discontinuities among young Christians' understanding of survival as Christians worldwide. Some know what it means to live in a Christian community because they grew up in the environment. Others are learning what it means to be Christian through social media, television shows, movies, and the Christians they encounter in the world around them.

It is crucial that churches and Christlike leaders learn and equip others on how to arm individuals with the tools to discern what they are already viewing as spiritual formation. The armor will help guard against some of the dangers that Christian film critics are conveying as concerns. Johnston recognizes, and I agree, that "movies have also proven to be a force for healing and insight. The power of film can change lives and communicate truth; it can reveal and redeem."[61] When the pop culture generation ceases to come to church for healing, insight, and redemption, where are they going? Some argue social media and streaming platforms are providing the spirituality that culture is searching for faithfully.

---

60. Hauerwas and Willimon, *Resident Aliens*, 150.
61. Johnston, *Reel Spirituality*, 24.

How will pop culture come to know the Christ of the church if the church is not a place sought to connect with anymore? Ryan Parker of the *Pop Theology* website shared in an interview with Cooperative Baptist Fellowship that pastors need to be culturally aware so that they may meet congregants where they are.[62] Films are a way to achieve the goal of connectedness. Parker also acknowledges films being a source of spiritual formation, and churches seizing the opportunity to watch films, Christian or not, is a ministry of being together with congregants and the community.[63] Generations raised today have yet lived in the Christian community long enough (if at all) to experience the reinforcement of their faith. Suppose the church does not learn and teach Christians how to redeem the power of film for spiritual development; there is a danger of losing them to such a cultural "competitor" as visual media considerably. Pop culture is pacing away from the church. Movies are a way to unite people as the church and go even further to teach people how to discern beyond the screen to develop their spiritual formation.

FILM INFORMING A NEW PERSPECTIVE AND PROCESS OF UNDERSTANDING

In his book *on Christian Social Innovation*, Former Duke Divinity School Dean L. Gregory Jones, offers insight that can be applied to Christians considering Christian-based films as a probable spiritual discipline.[64] Jones emphasizes how the Christian faith can influence the mindsets, practices, and social innovation traits to expand Christian witness and resources.[65] I am claiming that Christian-based films, as a prospective spiritual discipline, are a resource and means of spiritual and social innovation with the storytelling power to share the Gospel and transform lives for Christ. A Christian-based film and spiritual formation fusion can serve as a change agent, a force to sustain social value, and have entrepreneurship potential with the intent to develop strategies that will offer support to help humans (spiritually) flourish.

I agree with Jones as he introduces the importance of innovation. He claims there are too many complex, wicked, and hard challenges that we

---

62. Hale, "The Spiritual Discipline of Watching Film Together."
63. Hale, "The Spiritual Discipline of Watching Film Together," 34:53.
64. Jones, *Christian Social Innovation*, 2–3.
65. Jones, Christian Social Innovation, 4.

face in the world and as Christians, while having a single approach to address them is not realistic.[66] Finding innovative techniques that challenge the norm—something new or limited—is necessary to serve with efficacy.[67] Intentionally incorporating Christian-based films into the practice of spiritual formation is the approach that has inspired me to explore further practical use, realizing the truth behind Jones' point. As a Christ-like leader, I am studying social and spiritual innovation in evaluating how Christian-based films and spiritual formation can be intentionally transformative for those willing to engage in both practices simultaneously. All Christian leadership was called beyond the church walls even before the global pandemic forced pastors and religious leaders to focus outside their buildings. My ministry, Essence of Love Ministries (EofL), centers around creativity and imagination. The ministry serves to equip and disciple through creative writing platforms, films, social gatherings, and events that are not present or sustainable at churches in the areas we serve. Just as the churches were challenged in conducting "church business as usual," I had to determine how my ministry would need to evolve in light of a global pandemic and continuing post-pandemic that hindered social gatherings and in-person events. As hosting groups to watch Christian-based movies at the theater and having dinner discussions at restaurants afterward was a feature program of EofL, I prayed to discern how I could continue to utilize film as a spiritual development tool. The process of introspection of social and spiritual innovation has led to a new perspective, approach to understanding, and ultimately to the subject of my central argument.

Mindset is essential to ministry and social innovation, especially as a Christian. In everything we do as Christians, we bring the perspective of Jesus Christ and our own witness as disciples making more disciples.[68] The thought supports T.C. Stalling's view of remaining aligned with Jesus and Scripture when communicating through the medium of film.[69] Christian minds should be set on practicing the traditional or classic spiritual disciplines that Richard Foster recognizes in *Celebration of Discipline*. The church buildings and places of worship need to be supported, attended, and treasured by the Body of Christ as a beacon drawing us "home" together as the family of Christ. The fellowship of believers fuels us to go

---

66. Jones, Christian Social Innovation, 1.
67. Jones, Christian Social Innovation, 3.
68. Jones, *Christian Social Innovation*, 4.
69. *Faith On Film #112*, 14:40–16:10.

back into the world and invite others to return with us as disciples. Our Christian traditions have purpose and value, and we should always create space to keep them present and active. With that said, we also must give great room for new perspectives and innovative ways to pass on our Christian traditions to cultivate the efficacy of fulfilling the mandate given by Jesus to make more disciples.

Currently, the church has to deal with the challenges of declining attendance. Where do we reach the people if the church cannot preach, teach, spiritually nourish, and gather in fellowship with people in its edifices? Who influences spiritual growth and ensures what people learn is Gospel truth if not connected to the church? How do we support their spiritual searching and guide them to discover connection points with God? What will become of practicing the traditional spiritual disciplines if Christians do not understand that overlooked spiritual disciplines can influence the enhancement of the traditional ones? All these questions must rest at the altar of prayer with surrender and an embrace of how God will provide the answers. As I present my core idea, Christian-based movies serve as an answer, offering a new perspective on the potential ways Christians can spiritually grow and deepen their relationship with Jesus Christ, presenting it as a viable spiritual discipline. Although the perspective is not technically new, as Christians, we need to examine our standpoint and understand how God is calling the church to adjust to share the story of Christ in this visual media era of popular culture. Looking on from the vantage point of Dallas Willard, spiritual disciplines are where we are and what we do every day, fully connecting us to the enjoyment and love of God.[70] However, Willard's point of view may challenge some people's perspectives. Screen stories are a means to share, teach, and spread the Gospel. The end result is to make more disciples, guide them in the way of Christ, and share with the world that Jesus desires a relationship with them. Using Christian-based films is a method available where people are already gathering and an activity they are doing relatively every day. Having acknowledged and discussed the essential role film plays in shaping our culture and thus our responsibility as Christians to take its influence seriously, we now must explore how Christian-based movies portray the Scriptures for spiritual formation.

---

70. Willard, *The Spirit of the Disciplines*, 137.

RECOGNIZING AND UNDERSTANDING BIBLICAL THEMES IN CHRISTIAN-BASED FILMS

Having your Bible in hand is essential to engaging Christian-based films as a possible spiritual discipline. The Scriptures are always the guide to understanding the biblical truth, along with the guidance of the Holy Spirit when discerning the theological and spiritual messages a Christian-based film conveys to viewers. In *Bible and Film*, Matthew Rindge discusses how the inclusion of biblical material in films contributes to the narrative's meaning and may prompt people to rethink and reconsider the meaning of a biblical text.[71] However, he is referencing films that are not classified specifically as Christian-based films as I am in my central argument claim.

Understanding biblical themes in Christian-based films is essential to the process of spiritual formation, as the objective is to be formed into the likeness of Christ. When biblical themes or text are included in a Christian-based film (and I say with conviction that Scripture should be used to categorize a film as Christian), the Scriptures help shape the narrative and expected end to the story. The dramatization of the Scriptures or the inspiration of telling stories that emphasize a message or lesson from Scripture is a way to lead viewers to discern, think, imagine, or consider what the Holy Spirit is communicating to them at the moment.

Various themes in Christian-based films may present or challenge viewers in understanding the Triune God's identity. *The Shack* is a prime example of how the holy imagination of screen stories can cause us to reimagine the Scriptures and understand biblical themes. God (Papa) was portrayed initially as an African American woman (Octavia Spencer) and later as an Indigenous man (Graham Greene) to dramatize that God was a mother to Mack (Sam Worthington) when he had a lack of trust for a father figure in his life. When Mack reached the point of forgiving his father (Derek Hamilton), Papa became the male personification of God because Mack was receptive to trusting a male representation of Papa.

As observed in the previous chapter, critics of the film took issue with the movie's presentation of God as a woman (also a Black woman) and an Indigenous man. The underlying issues in the criticism are flawed biblical interpretation, cultural bias, and racism that continue to plague our global society. What is conveyed in the movie is that Jehovah will show up in the necessary form required to reach the lost and broken-hearted, have

---

71. Rindge, *Bible and Film*, 111–39.

a relationship, and care for them. When we consider Scripture, the idea points to how the Lord will receive (take care of) those whose father or mother has forsaken them (or not in their lives).[72] Amy Simpson, managing editor of *Today's Christian Woman*, outlines the biblical references of where God is likened to a woman or mother for further insight.[73]

The Shack either comforted, caused people to rethink, or have an adverse reaction to God portrayed as a female or a culture different from what they had been taught by their churches, spiritual leaders, or cultural interpretations of Scripture. The same goes for the film's portrayal of Jesus (Aviv Alush) as a Palestinian Jew with dark hair and brown eyes and the Holy Spirit called Sarayu (Sumire), translated to mean air or wind, played by an Asian woman. The identity of the Triune God is beyond our understanding. As we read the Scriptures and understand that we are all made in the Imago Dei, reimagining God being presented in the form to work beyond the barriers to reach the hearts of humanity should not be controversial but embraced. Movies have the power to take us on a reimagining journey that helps us grow spiritually closer to the Triune God. Spiritual disciplines exist to aid us in our efforts to do so.

When the Kendrick Brothers produced the movie *War Room*, biblical themes were evident in their intentions for the film. As the screen story plays out, it is undergirded by a core scriptural reference found in 2 Chronicles 7:14, "if my people who are called by my name humble themselves, pray, seek my face, and turn from their wicked ways, then I will hear from heaven and will forgive their sin and heal their land."[74] As discussed in chapter 1, the power of prayer and knowing Scripture with conviction are two biblical themes communicated in *War Room*. James 5:16 says, "Therefore confess your sins to one another and pray for one another, so that you may be healed. The prayer of the righteous is powerful and effective."[75] The film intentionally influences viewers to assess and grow in the spiritual discipline of prayer and believe that the prayers of the righteous produce results. As with any film, Christian or non-Christian, *War Room* had critics who thought that the results of some of the prayers in the movie were drastic or unrealistic. I would say that to think that God cannot do the impossible warrants concern for the body of believers in Jesus Christ because

---

72. Ps 27:10; 68:5.
73. Sampson, "Mother to the Motherless."
74. 2 Chr 7:14 (NRSVUE).
75. Jas 5:16 (NRSVUE).

the Bible is full of "drastic" acts and "unrealistic" miracles. Although there are answers to prayers in the film that may appear overly "dramatized" to some, others may feel empowered and encouraged to believe that God hears their prayers and will answer as the Scriptures witness to us from Genesis through Revelation.

The theme of prayer in the Bible for Christians is rooted in Jesus' model with the disciples in Matthew 6:9–13, also known as The Lord's Prayer. Jesus taught the disciples how to pray when they sought to better communicate with God after witnessing Jesus' prayer life with the Father. Throughout the Old and New Testaments, various characters directly or indirectly recognize, understand, and model prayer in communication with God. Movies that dramatize the biblical principles of prayer practice, process, and power help viewers identify, understand, grow, mature, and sustain inadvertently or advertently communication with God. Films have the ability to bring prayer and Scripture to life to model out what some may have difficulty understanding otherwise read, taught, preached, or imagined.

Engaging Christian-based films as a possible spiritual discipline, studying the Scriptures, and praying for discernment are necessary to recognize and understand biblical themes. In viewing Christian-based films as a viable spiritual discipline, practitioners must discern when the biblical themes are accurately and appropriately represented or interpreted. The film's theology must be considered and evaluated along with the Scriptures to determine if a film's message is true to the text, made with holy imagination, or leaning towards blasphemy. Christian-based films can take biblical themes and the ambiguity of what is not present in Scripture and create space for the Holy Spirit to connect and lead viewers to the biblical text. Movies give a great deal of space to explore the holy imagination. Films can fill in the gaps of biblical stories, leaving many concluding that there is more to the story and offering cinematic creative answers to what may lie in between what was untold. The imaginative spaces in between that are brought to life through films are powerful tools as a viable spiritual discipline, possibly giving way to making a relatable experience that may lead to a divine encounter.

The Passion of the Christ (2004) is a prime example of imaginative space used to fill in the gaps of the four Gospels telling the story of the crucifixion of Jesus. Several Passion plays have dramatized the historic event with various unfavorable and favorable critical responses. In Mel Gibson's Passion version, he not only weaves together the Gospels but uses nonbiblical references and his religious and cultural biases to build the story of his version of the biblical account. One example of Gibson weaving together biblical themes is in Satan's presence throughout the film. The adversary often lurks in the background, but the Gospels do not record such an explicit presence. His emphasis on the devil is not excessive because the Bible states Satan as God's and our adversary from Genesis to Revelation.[76] Gibson brings to viewers' attention how Satan is always prowling in the background helps remind us that we have a persistent enemy that we cannot see.

Various controversial biblical messaging of Gibson's dramatization led Christian and Jewish scholars to evaluate the film's biblical accuracy.[77] Concerns of anti-Semitism to the crucifixion's violent display have been controversial topics related to the movie. Such responses may warrant caution for some viewers. At the same time, *The Passion of the Christ* rates as one of the highest-grossing Christian-themed movies in history.[78] Whether or not Christian leaders, scholars, or laypersons deem the movie culturally harmful or biblically inaccurate, people have flocked to theaters to view the film. We cannot stop people from viewing accurate or flawed messages represented in Christian-based films. Knowing this fact, Christians would do well becoming equipped to address and engage viewers with the truth and tools to discern the truth found in Scripture. Jesuit priest and film critic Richard Leonard, SJ, offers more details surrounding the controversy Gibson's version of the film has kept in toll. Using *The Passion of the Christ* as an example of the importance of understanding and recognizing biblical themes in Christian-based films shows the need-to-know Scripture, the filmmakers' influences/references for creating the film, and discern what is fact or imagination in their dramatized depiction of the biblical stories. Leonard also provides insight into Mel Gibson's use of *The Dolorous Passion of Our Lord Jesus Christ* by Anne Catherine Emmerich to influence the way he told the story of the Passion.[79] Cultivating spiritual development with a fortified foundation of Christian theology and the Gospel truth will support utilizing Christian-based films as a possible spiritual discipline.

---

76. 1 Pet 5:7–9 later notes that the devil is roaming and seeking to devour people of the faith.
77. Garber, *Mel Gibson's Passion*.
78. Fuster, "10 Highest Grossing Christian-Themed Movies."
79. Leonard, *Movies that Matter*, 150–54.

DISCERNING SPIRITUALITY IN CHRISTIAN-BASED FILMS

Spirituality is understood as a search or practice of faith hoping to connect with something greater than ourselves. In the process of Christian spiritual formation, practitioners are always seeking to make a spiritual connection with the Triune God. Spiritual disciplines are tools to help believers in Jesus Christ connect to him, learn more about him, and become equipped to live a life as a disciple of Christ with the help of the Holy Spirit. How can movies help seekers (those searching for spirituality) and believers (followers of Christ) in their spirituality? As Plantinga asserts, "Screen stories, more easily than word stories, cross the boundaries of nation and language, literate and illiterate, class, income, and level of education."[80] Film crossing boundaries opens the way (or imagination) for diverse groups of people seeking to find a connection to something greater than themselves, meaning in their existence, and answers to life's complexities. Christian and non-Christian-based films have the power to speak to viewers with the eyes to see spiritually and ears to hear. Many people do not intend to go to the movies seeking a spiritual experience and have one, for that matter.

In some cases, people have watched films and had the unexpected transcendent experience that Johnston speaks of in *Reel Spirituality*. I would say those people who do have a divine encounter are most likely the ones who have been searching for spiritual understanding and a connection beyond themselves. As films have the tenets to cross cultural boundaries, equipping viewers to recognize and discern the messages of spirituality in the movies they are watching is beneficial for spiritual understanding and growth.

Expanding on the spiritual formation teachings by Lynda L. Graybeal and Julia L. Roller, one form of becoming spiritually developed is in the practice of spiritual disciplines.[81] Graybeal and Roller first introduce the understanding of the "with God" life principle of Renovaré. The term is derived from the "Immanuel Principle" of life, meaning "the unity of the Bible is discovered in the development of life with God as a reality on earth, centered in the person of Jesus."[82] Renovaré refers to the understanding of holistic Christlikeness as the "with-God" life, transforming the whole

---

80. Plantinga, *Power of Screen Stories*, 17.
81. Graybeal and Roller, *Learning from Jesus*.
82. Graybeal and Roller, *Learning from Jesus*, xi.

person and whole life.[83] As was noted previously, the Renovaré Institute seeks to guide and enable those who participate in their practical tools to see, understand, and to experience Christlikeness in every area of their lives.[84]

In the "with-God" life process, Graybeal and Roller emphasize that those who practice the spiritual principle must be open and prepared to have a biblical exploration that may question the fundamentals that we have held close to heart and have been foundational to our faith.[85] They point out that all disciplines are built upon Scripture, and our practice of spiritual disciplines remains aligned with the scripture as we frequently engage the Word of God.[86] In studying the Scriptures, we see the way Jesus lived and interacted with human beings. With the openness that Graybeal and Roller lay as a foundation for spiritual transformation, they say we will find ways to allow Jesus to live in every dimension of our lives in the daily process.[87]

> We begin by finding experientially, day by day, how to let Jesus Christ live in every dimension of our being. In Christian community, we can open our lives to God's life by gathering regularly in little groups of two or more to encourage one another to discover the footprints of God in our daily existence and to venture out with God into areas where we have previously walked alone or not at all. But the aim is not external conformity, whether to doctrine or deed, but the re-formation of the inner self—of the spiritual core, the place of thought and feeling, of will and character.[88]

The movie theater or watching films is one of the areas that I present as a place that we often walk alone, and others may not enter at all when searching for God to build or sustain a prospering relationship. For those who may object to the thought that God cannot be searched for and found in watching television or a movie, I would offer consideration of the Renovaré concept of the "with-God" life. Also, studying the Scriptures to see the places Jesus dared to go when others would not or did the incomprehensible for the generation he walked among in the flesh.

---

83. Graybeal and Roller, *Learning from Jesus*, xi.
84. Graybeal and Roller, *Learning from Jesus*, xi.
85. Graybeal and Roller, *Learning from Jesus*, xi.
86. Graybeal and Roller, *Learning from Jesus*, xii.
87. Graybeal and Roller, Learning from Jesus, xii.
88. Graybeal and Roller, *Learning from Jesus*, xii.

Establishment and Flourishing of Cinema's Influence

As I present watching Christian-based films in alignment with the Gospel of Jesus Christ and the Holy Bible as a viable spiritual discipline, I want to mark the thought of Graybeal and Roller as being open to experiencing God in the places and spaces we may overlook. I say that omitting the visual media genre from the list of spiritual disciplines is an oversight that can no longer be ignored or not taken seriously with consideration of incorporation. Some may challenge screen stories being grafted into the list of spiritual disciplines because they are not found in Scripture. The people challenging the concept can stand supported by interpreting Graybeal and Roller's statement that all spiritual disciplines are rooted in the Scripture. I would counter the challenge by stating that movies (screen stories) are the dramatized parables (stories) that have evolved from the oral tradition that Jesus practiced (evident in Scripture) to the innovation of visual media storytelling we are accustomed to in our society today.

Relating to Christian-based films, I would conclude that many of those choosing to watch the genre of movies expect a spiritual experience that affirms, challenges, or strengthens their faith. In this case, discernment is necessary and critical to how the film is used as a viable spiritual discipline to help in spiritual formation with the intent to grow closer to Jesus Christ and spiritually flourish. How can one discern spirituality in a Christian-based film? The answer is whether the film leads the viewers to connect, build, or sustain a relationship with Jesus Christ while foundational in Scripture. Also, the faith community should not be disregarded in the discernment process because the Holy Spirit dwells within the Body of Christ. Johnston, Detweiler, and Callaway add to the subject, saying, "discernment is always needed, and for this reason maintaining an interpretive community is so important. We need the perspective of the "other" to appreciate before we appraise. That appreciation takes film seriously as a potential source for revelatory insight before we too quickly condemn it (and each other) either as a subversion of the gospel, as heretical, or worst of all (!), as 'unbiblical.'"[89] As the Body of Christ, each member is given spiritual gifts to glorify God and edify the family of Christ. Those gifted with the spiritual gifts of wisdom, knowledge, and discernment called to the ministry of film criticism can be beneficial in equipping believers (and discipleship strategies) in viewing films as a possible spiritual discipline.[90]

---

89. Johnston, et al., *Deep Focus*, 199.

90. Bugbee and Cousins, *Network Participant's Guide* and Bugbee, *Discover Your Spiritual Gifts*.

Discerning Beyond the Screen

I must re-emphasize the role of the Holy Spirit in discerning the who, what, when, where, and how the Lord is seeking to connect with viewers open to embrace a divine encounter by watching a movie. A biopic Christian-based film highlights spirituality based on a true story. The screen stories often demonstrate the individuals' and community's spiritual formation, influence, and development. *Breakthrough* (2019) is a screen story that recounts the miraculous events surrounding the life of John Smith (Marcel Ruiz) after falling into a frozen lake and drowning after being trapped for fifteen minutes in the water. The categorized faith-based biopic film is considered a Christian-based movie because the focus is belief in the Lord Jesus Christ; faith that Jesus has the power to bring John back to life after being declared dead. John's mother, Joyce (Chrissy Metz), refuses to accept the doctor's report and prays for God to send the Holy Spirit to save her son.[91] Miraculously, her prayer was answered as the monitors indicated John's reviving pulse, and everyone witnessed life return to John. As the events unfold to Joyce's answered prayer, John, his parents, family, friends, and the entire community experience their spirituality being discovered, challenged, and solidified; unifying through faith, hope, and love rooted in Jesus Christ.

If there had not been witnesses to John Smith's miraculous story, many would not have believed that the events took place, but they did. The spiritual journey of John, his family, and the St. Louis community was created into a faith-based film for the world to witness. Their story of faith reached and led people near and far to Jesus Christ, longing for something to believe in beyond themselves. Actor Josh Lucas shared that the expression of spirituality (faith) expressed by the community singing outside John's hospital room was a key influence in his choosing to play the role of John's father, Brian Smith, in the movie.[92] Lucas goes on to share that after telling his six-year-old son the story of the community singing outside the hospital, his son's discerning voice telling him to do the movie was the confirmation he needed to accept the part of Brian Smith. The exact spiritual moment that influenced Josh Lucas and his son is displayed in the film as a witness to a community's spirituality.

Lucas does not mention that the Holy Spirit influenced him or his son after being exposed to the story of a community's faith in action. However, the moving of the Holy Spirit is discerned in the process of bringing the

---

91. Dawson, *Breakthrough*.
92. BUILD Series, "Josh Lucas Encourages Audiences."

film's production together. The lead producer for the film is Devon Franklin, who is also a Christian and minister of the Gospel. Johnston, Detweiler, and Callaway say that "our pneumatology matters. Because the Spirit who confronts us in the cinema is the very same Spirit who draws together the people of God, our willingness to encounter the cultural, religious, and racial other in and through film must also apply to the other we encounter within the body of Christ."[93] Films that express the Christian foundations of spirituality can be spiritual discipline tools for the faith community personally and corporately for discerning how to spiritually navigate life and disciple those seeking to make a connection and grow closer to Jesus Christ, advertently or inadvertently.

THE TRANSCENDENCE OF FILM AND SPIRITUALITY DEVELOPING SPIRITUAL FORMATION

To engage a Christian-based film as a viable spiritual discipline (to support spiritual growth and deepen our relationship with Jesus Christ), we must approach viewing with discernment with the hopes of experiencing spiritual transcendence to nurture our spiritual formation development. How does watching a Christian-based film contribute to developing spiritual formation with the desire to deepen one's relationship with Jesus Christ and spiritually grow? When observing the insights of film history, theologians, ethicists, pastoral leaders, film critics, and psychologists, most agree that movies have the power to influence viewers. However, their arguments tend to differ on film's powerful influence being a positive or negative factor on popular culture or developing a viewer's morals and spiritual growth. All perspectives that each movie critic brings, while open to embracing the "full integrity" of the film, have valid points of concern and caution or persuasive consideration regarding how film can lead to transcendence. In weighing all perspectives of scholars, religious leaders, and film professionals, I have concluded that with intentional equipping as a viable spiritual discipline, screen stories can engage all of a person's senses and produce congruence leading to transcendence and spiritual development.

People long to have a connection with a higher power for several reasons. Some reasons may be to find identity, purpose, hope, understanding, peace, fulfillment, or support for overall well-being. When people are on their spiritual journey, they mindfully and soulfully search for transcendent

---

93. Johnston, et al., *Deep Focus*, 199.

experiences often found in unexpected people, places, things, and ways. I agree that going to the cinema or streaming a movie on a technological device has proven to be an unexpected entity in which spiritual connections have been made and developed. For Christians, choosing to watch a Christian or faith-based movie is often because of their spiritual relationship with Jesus Christ. A Christian choosing a faith-based film does not often consider the aesthetics, spiritual fluff, unrealistic or miraculous events, or poor performances that critics tend to highlight. Christians search for a spiritual connection through dramatized storytelling, often not found in routine Christian practices or disciplines. Some Christians may watch a faith-based movie for enjoyment appropriate for the entire family to watch, interest in the thematic message marketed, or in hopes of working through faith challenges they are experiencing. In proposing that a follower of Christ watch a Christian-based film as a possible spiritual discipline, I am suggesting that the practice can simultaneously engage multiple senses guided by the Holy Spirit to experience a divine encounter or spiritual awareness. I also recognize that harmoniously engaging several senses is not the only possibility for transcendence. Just as significantly, Christian-based films are a creative means to incorporate multiple spiritual discipline practices (i.e., prayer, fasting, study, meditation, celebration, etc.) in one cinematic viewing to synchronize the spiritual formation process for participants. The transcendence or spiritual awareness from the experience that leads to spiritual growth or a deepened relationship with Jesus Christ is the hope and intention of viewing the films as a viable spiritual discipline for developing the spiritual formation process.

Every spiritual discipline is in place as a tool to nurture spiritual growth in those who choose to follow Jesus Christ. Spiritual disciplines have the inward and outward undergirding to spiritually guide and form us as individuals and as a faith community called to live as disciples of Jesus Christ. Watching films is not a pleasurable means of leisure, worthy of time or consideration, or fathomable as a spiritual tool to numerous Christians. However, I believe that most Christians in the twenty-first century are keenly aware that movies are a powerful source to influence the world with the message of the Gospel as Christian-based film productions continue to grow. The Christian skeptics who are still challenged by the Christian-based film movement may wonder how God can use film for our good and God's glory. My central argument urges skeptics and supporters of cinema to be more intentional in exploring, learning, teaching, and using Christian-based films as a possible spiritual discipline.

Christian-based films can reach a place within us that has been hard to find or complicated to reach to build a connection we have spiritually longed to encounter with the Triune God. God is sovereign and has the power to choose how to reveal God's self to humanity.[94] For anyone from any background, belief, discipline of study, doctrine, profession, culture, or the like to determine that God cannot and will not use screen stories to connect with human beings and build a relationship, they are our current culture's Pharisees and Sadducees. The religious and secular Christian and faith-based film critics discrediting screen stories do not have the discerning eyes to see and ears to hear just how God is reaching people outside the church's four walls. God is calling for a generation that no longer seeks to enter the House of the Lord for a divine encounter but still longs for a spiritual connection leading to transcendence. Johnston, Detweiler, and Callaway form my last thought in this way, "film might well become in God's mysterious plan the vehicle by which God speaks to those both within and outside the church."[95]

---

94. Johnston, et al., *Deep Focus*, 153.
95. Johnston, et al., *Deep Focus*, 153.

Chapter Four

Embracing Christian-based Films as a Prospective Spiritual Discipline

THE PROCESS OF EMBRACING Christian-based films as a possible spiritual discipline requires a fundamental understanding of the need to openly posture ourselves to the revelations of the Holy Spirit. Surrendering to the Holy Spirit's influence through the storytelling of Christian-based films can spiritually form us by cultivating spiritual growth and a deeper relationship with Jesus Christ. When observing the previous chapters on spiritual formation, storytelling, and the various distinctions of film's connection to spirituality, three areas are essential to embracing Christian-based films as a potential spiritual discipline. The first component that the central argument needs to establish is recognizing films as a means of storytelling. Storytelling has been God's way of communicating with humanity throughout history, how we communicate with each other, and the evolution of storytelling has significantly impacted popular culture. The second element essential to embracing Christian-based film as a possible spiritual discipline is the need to be guided by spiritual discernment. The discernment of having the eyes to see and ears to hear what the Lord is communicating to us through screen stories opens the way to spiritual formation and transcendence practiced as a potential spiritual discipline. The third factor undergirding the central argument is that the movies we watch influence a response. No matter the genre of films we are engaging in, we are being influenced to respond positively, negatively, or transcendently.

Embracing Christian-based Films

To embrace Christian-based screen stories as a potential spiritual discipline, the results must be to obtain spiritual growth or a closer relationship with Jesus Christ. As detailed in chapter 1, the spiritual disciplines in a traditional sense are those practices found in the Scriptures modeled by Jesus Christ and taught to his Apostles and disciples. Spiritual disciplines are practices that nurture spiritual growth, are training tools to bring about spiritual maturity, and ways that sustain the connection we have with God as followers of Jesus Christ. Over time, spiritual formation scholars and practitioners, taking on the vantage point of Dallas Willard, have recognized that "spiritual disciplines are the exercises or activities that enable us to receive more of Christ and his power without harming ourselves or others."[1] Concerning Willard's distinction of what a spiritual discipline is and the purpose of its function, I make a case for Christian-based films becoming classified as a viable spiritual discipline. Along with Willard's adaptation of how we recognize a practice as a spiritual discipline, the method of storytelling is the spiritual practice often used in Scripture but not incorporated as a discipline. The two entities give way to Christian-based films to enter the category of a spiritual discipline practice, fortifying the pillars of support examined in the chosen method Jesus used to reach, teach, and transform his hearers for spiritual formation through the means of storytelling.

When Christian-based films have the foundational principles of a spiritual discipline, the genre should be incorporated into the spiritual practice. If watching screen stories sows the seed of the Gospel of Jesus Christ, nurtures and sustains spiritual growth, and strengthens a believer's relationship with Jesus Christ, enabling them to live as a disciple consistently aligning with Scripture, then the practice constitutes a spiritual discipline. How do Christian-based films accomplish the goal of a spiritual discipline? How do we discern the Holy Spirit using screen stories to transform us in the spiritual formation process? I have developed a framework to outline how Christian-based films function as a viable spiritual discipline. I will analyze three films (fiction, biopic, and biblically-based) to demonstrate how they are a likely spiritual discipline. I have presented, evaluated, and substantiated the reasons Christian-based films are considered a spiritual discipline. Moving forward, I introduce the conceptual framework to demonstrate how the visual media genre can be used as a means of spiritual growth and to deepen a relationship with Jesus Christ in the lives of those engaging in spiritual formation. I will then model the framework by analyzing how the three Christian-based films I have selected implement the goals of a

---

1. Willard, *The Spirit of the Disciplines*, 156.

spiritual discipline as they communicate the Gospel of Jesus Christ and the attributes of a disciple of Christ as Jesus has taught. Next, I will examine the necessity to recognize how the Holy Spirit communicates through the films for spiritual growth and to nurture a deeper relationship with Jesus Christ. In evaluating the Christian story conveyed through the films with spiritual discernment, I will observe how the films influence a response that can include an experience of transcendence that leads to transformation. The transformation expected is in the goal of a spiritual discipline, which is to promote spiritual growth and deepen a relationship with Jesus Christ. I will also assess how the films have the potential to transform us in the spiritual formation process and move us to discipleship.

CHRISTIAN-BASED FILMS AS A VIABLE SPIRITUAL DISCIPLINE FRAMEWORK

Christian-based films have the capacity to support spiritual growth and deepen our relationship with Jesus Christ, but how? The central argument has explored the impact storytelling has had in spiritually forming and guiding people since Creation into today's popular culture. Cinema has been among the evolution of storytelling since its introduction in the late 1800s. The genre has advanced to the present-day creative phenomenon that moving picture inventors could have never imagined. If we believe as followers of Christ that God is in all things and is using all things to bring about revelation, then storytelling through the projection of movies is inclusive of God's sources of reaching humanity.

How can screen stories be God working all things for good and instruments in our spiritual toolbox to reach people's hearts? A conclusion that I make, based on the psychology, theology, spirituality, and cultural influence of film's power, is that movies demand viewers to respond to the stories being shared on the screen. Chapter 3 presents a connection on how our brains are wired to respond to storytelling. In the connection, the central argument engages how we have been taught to live and what to believe spiritually and culturally that forms or challenges our theology. Screen stories that impact the way we see, think, and feel about messages being portrayed form part of a process that moves us to consider a negative or positive response directly impacting our lives.

The dramatization of life relative to our own, flashing before our eyes and tugging at our hearts, gives way to the Holy Spirit to transform us miraculously. Each step in the process, from the start of a film to its ending, can potentially bring us to spiritual maturity. The interaction of the Holy Spirit working within believers embracing Christian-based films as a possible spiritual discipline with discernment positions us to surrender our logic and allow for a transcendent experience. As we spiritually grow, we deepen our relationship with Jesus Christ with the eyes to see and ears to hear what God is communicating with us as we discern beyond the silver screens. As a result of the spiritual growth and increased intimacy with Jesus Christ, we will heed his command to go and make disciples of all nations as evidence of our spiritual transformation.[2]

Modern-day storytelling through screen stories can be a powerful and influential tool in spiritual formation. When we approach Christian-based movies with spiritual discernment, a transcendent response is possible through the power of the Holy Spirit at work in us. In the process, film can become a viable spiritual discipline leading to a way of discipleship. As I examine the movies, *A Question of Faith* (2017), *Soul Surfer* (2011), and *Son of God* (2014), I will do so by modeling the framework of viewing the films as a probable spiritual discipline that nurtures spiritual growth and deepens a relationship with Jesus Christ. Additionally, I will discuss how the films provide a resource for discipleship within the process, prompting viewers to reflect Christlike behavior as they have been taught.

SPIRITUAL DISCIPLINE MODEL FOR CHRISTIAN-BASED FILMS

Diagram 1 illustrates the framework I will use to analyze the three Christian-based films as a viable spiritual discipline. The framework offers insight and guidance on how films can be a tool to nurture spiritual growth and strengthen a relationship with Jesus Christ. In *Deep Focus*, the authors shared how Craig Detweiler's film analysis professor, Frank Daniel, at the University of Southern California, provided a simple and effective structure for analyzing stories. The model was outlined to include watching the film twice within two weeks, dissecting the story, and outlining every act, sequence, and scene. I will consider Daniel's model in recognizing the cinematic structure of the films I am examining.[3]

---

2. Matt 28:19–20 (NRSVUE).
3. Johnston, et al., *Deep Focus*, 60–61.

Diagram 1: Framework for Viewing Christian-based Films as a Spiritual Discipline

As I present the model of Christian-based films as a viable spiritual discipline, I intentionally do so through the flow of each step in the framework. The framework creates space for the Holy Spirit in the process that I will be unable to quantify in my analysis. Still, I recognize the necessity of the Holy Spirit's inclusion in the process. In the case of viewing Christian-based films (or in all film viewing) and practicing the traditional spiritual disciplines, we rely on the Holy Spirit to have a transcendental encounter and experience spiritual transformation. This is admittedly just one possible model to achieve the goal of spiritual growth and a deeper relationship with Jesus Christ.

With the purpose in mind, the first step is determining if the chosen film is considered Christian-based. I define the Christian-based genre as fiction and non-fiction screen stories centered on telling the story of Christ, his teachings, and the lives of believers connected to both areas. In understanding the goal of a spiritual discipline, to nurture spiritual growth and a deeper relationship with Jesus Christ, the elements within the definition must be present in the films. Recognizing that films that are considered faith-based and inspirational can also be tools used in the spiritual discipline process is necessary to point out. There may also be films that represent Christ-figure characters or themes that may accomplish the purpose of a spiritual discipline as well. I am reiterating film theologians' conclusions that God can speak through any genre of films to reach the hearts of people; however, my focus is solely on Christian-based films for the central argument.

In selecting the movie, critical reviews, doctrine, biases, and many internal or external influences may cause doubt about whether or not the film is beneficial for the spiritual formation process. In either case, I agree with Robert Johnston in allowing the film to communicate with its full integrity.[4] In the best conceivable way, having the ability to release preconceived thoughts, influences, and doctrines will help us move out of the way and surrender to the message the Holy Spirit is sharing with us. Surrendering to the Holy Spirit is the second step in the process that is essential to reach the objective of films achieving the aim of a spiritual discipline. Also, when viewing a Christian-based movie, preparing to discern is necessary to test messaging against Scripture so as not to be influenced by any form of evil that will lead away from the intended goal of spiritual growth and nurturing a deeper relationship with Jesus Christ. With this in mind, it is important to prepare ourselves for viewing screen stories by testing everything against Scripture and remember: "Do not quench the Spirit. Do not despise prophecies, but test everything; hold fast to what is good; abstain from every form of evil."[5]

---

4. Johnston, *Reel Spirituality*, 100.
5. 1 Thess 5:19–22 (NRSVUE).

Discerning Beyond the Screen

The third phase of the process is acknowledging the three essential areas I previously mentioned for films to be considered a spiritual discipline in the central argument. Once again, the three critical components are to be able to: 1) acknowledge film as storytelling and identify the message of the Gospel and teachings of Jesus Christ that are being communicated in the screen story, 2) grow in spiritual discernment through the posture of prayer to have the eyes to see and ears to hear what the Holy Spirit is communicating through the screen story, and 3) remaining aware how the film is influencing a response from you that may range from positive to negative with the potential to lead to transcendence or transformation personally or corporately. Recognizing the psychological impacts storytelling has on our brains, as outlined in chapter 2, all of our traditional senses are engaged as a story is told, causing us to react to what we imaginatively see, hear, taste, touch, and smell. Screen stories have the power to connect with our emotions, intellect, and understanding of our lives, beliefs, circumstances, and the world—both past, present, and future. They have the power of influence to bring about transformation. Films provide the space to work out similar or alternative scenarios that we may or may not relate to, influencing how we will move forward in our lives. Movies are dramatized storytelling that has the means to entertain, educate, evoke, and mobilize people toward transformation through imagination. Imagination is a gift God created and gifted to human beings to move us beyond logic and perceive the possibility of something beyond ourselves. When imagination is expressed through storytelling, connections are made that form bonds that are transcendent. As we look at the bond that the church is struggling to create in discipling popular culture, Johnston acknowledges the consistency of transcendence cinema has on viewers that the church is lacking. In discussing film's story, Johnston quotes Ken Gire, acknowledging film being more consistent in offering transcendental experiences than the church.[6]

The elements that film contributes to transcendence are worth investigating as a discipleship tool. When considering all these things, Christian-based films influence a spiritual connection with viewers through entertainment to communicate, educate, evoke, and mobilize discerning hearts to spiritual growth and a deeper relationship with Jesus Christ. Paul advises that we not be conformed to the world that we live in but to discern what God's will is that is considered good, acceptable, and perfect. Preceding the discernment process, we are told that our minds must be

---

6. Johnston, *Reel Spirituality*, 100.

Embracing Christian-based Films

transformed through renewal. Films have the components to take viewers through a renewal process that transforms their minds and the way they choose to live and see the world in alignment with God's will.[7] As screen stories have such a decisive engagement on our psyche, our minds can be renewed and transformed spiritually by intentionally utilizing them for spiritual formation.

THE ROLE OF DISCERNMENT VIEWING CHRISTIAN-BASED FILMS FOR SPIRITUAL FORMATION

The first three phases of embracing Christian-based films as a viable spiritual discipline are spiritually positioning viewers to receive with the same intentions Jesus used the parables in his ministry. Jesus used parables to convey his messages, knowing that not everyone would understand or want to understand his points. He emphasized that people did not understand and that their hearts rejected his stories because they could not discern the meaning. The Scriptures speak to the spiritual blindness that was to be expected. Jesus explained to the disciples why he spoke in parables, providing insight into the prophecy in Isaiah 6:9–10, which states that people would hear God's Word and not understand, and see God's works and not perceive, because of their hardened hearts. Ezekiel 12:2 also warns that people would live rebelliously, hindering them from seeing and hearing God and living in obedience to The Lord's will. Jesus recognized that the hearers' hearts were dull and unwilling to receive. However, his creative communication approach through storytelling had a way of strategically engaging people and subtly reaching hearts open to welcome his message.

Christian-based films, through the use of discernment, strategically engage viewers to subtly reach their hearts. This can lead to a transcendent response or transformation, fostering spiritual growth and a deeper relationship with Christ. This approach aligns with Jesus' intention of using parables. When persons prayerfully utilize Christian-based films as a potential spiritual discipline with the gift of discernment, they are blessed to not only understand the message the film is conveying but will gain greater insight. The deeper internal awareness can give a greater perspective concerning how they have been spiritually influenced to respond in a way that brings glory to God, works for their good, and builds up and encourages God's people.[8]

7. In Rom 12:2.
8. Rom 8:28 and 1 Thess 5:11.

The fourth phase of the framework is intentionally viewing Christian-based films as a likely spiritual discipline. Viewing Christian-based films for learning, becoming more acquainted with, or enhancing the practice of spiritual disciplines accomplishes the overall goal of a spiritual discipline. (This is what I seek to do in the section that follows). The fifth phase of the framework is spiritual growth and a deepened relationship with Jesus Christ as a result of the Holy Spirit working transcendence or transformation within us. Before reaching phase five, we must first identify how the movie works as a viable spiritual discipline in our spiritual formation and recognize how the screen story nurtures our spiritual growth and strengthens our relationship with Jesus Christ.

Again, a spiritual discipline's purpose is to help believers and followers of Jesus Christ strengthen their relationship with him and experience spiritual maturity. The evidence of our growth and relationship with Jesus Christ leads to the sixth phase of the framework in which we determine if and when the experience is prompting the next step of discipleship to 'go' and make more disciples as Jesus has commanded us to do. The entire process outlined in the framework connects back to the understanding that movies are not absent of God working through them as stories to reach the hearts of people. As the Holy Spirit is at work in us to translate the message that God intends for us to receive, all things are working for our good and God's glory. Beyond the interaction that is taking place between our good and God's glory, there is another opportunity that leads to building others up in discipleship.

The proposed framework has the entities to support spiritual growth and deepen our relationship with Jesus Christ. To engage and embrace Christian-based films as a viable spiritual discipline with intentionality, there must be guidance in place. The phases in the framework create a path to guide people using Christian-based movies on their spiritual formation journey. Also, the phases serve as checkpoints or guardrails to stay the course to experience spiritual growth.

FICTION, BIOPIC, AND BIBLICAL: CHRISTIAN-BASED FILMS STUDY

Based on the "Framework for Viewing Christian-based Films as a Viable Spiritual Discipline" and following the model outlining the framework, I will analyze three Christian-based films as viable spiritual disciplines. I have chosen three different film categories to demonstrate diverse perspectives of storytelling within the genre of Christian-based filmmaking that is beneficial to spiritual formation. The first film I examine is a fictional screen story, *A Question of Faith* (2017).[9] Fictional screen stories represent the types of parables Jesus told to the crowds who gathered to hear his storytelling. The stories do not depict actual events but pull from realistic possible situations that viewers can build a connection with and consider different perspectives prompting a reaction to change.

The second movie is based on a true story and is classified as a biopic Christian-based film, *Soul Surfer* (2011).[10] Including a biopic screen story offers a person's real-life testimony of their faith tested by adversity. In telling the story, viewers experience the process of spiritual growth and how a deeper relationship with Jesus Christ can be nurtured. In many cases, the biopic is fortified because the person(s) featured participates in the process and approval of making the film and the story it conveys.

The third Christian-based film, *Son of God* (2014) imaginatively retells the story of Christ according to Scripture.[11] The Bible does not provide every intricate detail of what took place, and because it does not do so, filmmakers use the privilege of imagination to create a story that fits and flows for the creation of a movie. However, when filmmakers portray the Scriptures differently from what the Holy Bible declares, it has the potential to skew people's interpretations incorrectly, which is another reason for concern. The imaginative gap fillers and the fictional stories portrayed could hinder the spiritual formation process as Christians question the accuracy and theology communicated in the screen stories. As I will show, *Son of God* at times exemplifies creative freedom and imagination going too far, but I still discern the screen story's value as a potential spiritual discipline. *Son of God* can teach us to know, study, discern, and understand what the Scriptures do and do not say about Jesus, his life, his ministry, and his teachings. Overall, giving attention to a biblically-based screen story, that intends to bring the Word of God to life for viewers as edutainment, is essential to understand the need to study the Scriptures and discern between facts and imaginative gap fillers.[12]

---

9. Otto, *A Question of Faith*.
10. McNamara, *Soul Surfer*.
11. Spencer, *Son of God*.
12. "Edutainment" is defined as entertainment that is designed to be educational.

Screen stories that are fiction, biopic, and biblically-based are in separate categories within the genre; however, the same questions are applicable in considering each one for spiritual formation. As a person views the film as a possible spiritual discipline, how can they experience spiritual growth by watching the characters navigate through the story? In what ways do the characters' process in deepening their relationship with God influence and provide a guide for those viewing seeking to do the same? What is the biblical basis for the message and the theological implications the film is attempting to present? The psychology, theology, and influence of Christian-based films must be observed when considering the genre as a possible spiritual discipline. With the previous thought in mind, answering the raised questions about the following three films may offer the tools to discern beyond the filmmakers' intentions. I will consider all perspectives when analyzing the three films while using the framework to model Christian-based films as a viable spiritual discipline. The hope is to embrace what the Holy Spirit communicates to individual viewers seeking to spiritually grow and deepen their relationship with Jesus Christ.

A Question of Faith (2017)—Fiction

A Question of Faith is more than a story that presents the complicated themes of tragedy, disappointments, heartbreak, racism, and guilt. The film also offers insight into how the characters move towards healing and begin to triumph over their challenges, presented in one hour and fifty-three minutes of viewing. The common thread to the characters overcoming all that they are faced with is how they recognize the mysterious hand of God moving in their lives to work all things together for their good and God's glory.[13]

The multi-layered screen story introduces viewers to a family-centered theme that simultaneously provides insight into three families of diverse backgrounds interconnected by a tragedy. The first family is a multi-generational African American Christian family (The Newman Family), the first family of their local church and leaders in the community whose faith is challenged by the death of their child (Eric) caused by a distracted teen driver. The second family is a White Christian family (The Danielson Family) of three. The family's faith is tested as the bitter and bigoted husband's business is struggling, the daughter's (Michelle) life and dreams are suddenly threatened due to a heart condition, and the wife's faith in God works

---

13. Rom 8:28 (NRSVUE).

to hold her family together. The third family (The Hernandez Family) presented is a Latina single mother who owns a restaurant and doing her best to raise her naive and college-bound teenage daughter (Maria), who is responsible for the tragic death of the Newman's youngest son.

The movie's opening scene presents the Scripture found in Psalm 34:17, "When the righteous cry for help, the Lord hears and rescues them from all their troubles."[14] There is a kismet connection as the tragic events connect the three families working through their trauma, directly and indirectly, related to Eric's (Caleb T. Thomas) death. The tragedy that had the potential to destroy each family ended up being the demonstration of how God can take a horrific event in our lives and work the situation for the good of everyone as they looked to God for help in their time of trouble. Viewers have the opportunity to witness the transformation that takes place in the lives of each family simultaneously as God's sovereign power and plan are revealed in their process of spiritual growth.

The Power of Film: The Ministry of Visual Influence

In some films, technology advances the power of psychological impact through split screens, giving viewers an insight into how multiple characters are processing a situation simultaneously. Another film technique, called cross-cutting, has a similar psychological influence by illustrating parallel storylines showing characters that are intertwined and dealing with the same situation simultaneously in a sequence of cutting to each character's experience as the story develops. In the cross-cutting technique, viewers can experience each character's process of emotions that are impacted by the exact cause with different effects. Doing so allows viewers to empathize emotionally with the characters and their emotional process in handling the dilemma presented. Moreso, the technique has the power to draw viewers into the story by building a relational bridge that they can relate to, process their own emotions, or release the tension that they may have towards a comparable situation by gaining a different perspective.

The Newman family is overwhelmed by grief and charting their way to their new normal to move forward after senselessly losing Eric to a car accident because of texting and driving. The loss of Eric's life is at the hands of Maria (Karen Valero), who was texting while driving when she hit Eric, eventually causing his death. At this point, the Hernandez family becomes

14. Ps 34:17 (NRSVUE).

an intricate piece woven into the connection between all three families. The Newmans decide to donate Eric's organs, which begins the process of connecting them to the Danielson family. The Danielson and Newman families' stories are paralleled as Michelle (Amber Nelon Thompson) becomes ill, needs a heart transplant, and receives Eric's heart. As the conflict presented in *A Question of Faith* weaves together all three families and those in a relationship with them, the powerful dynamics of film technology allow viewers to engage each family concurrently.

An example of the cross-cutting technique throughout the film is in the tragic event that initially weaves the three families together as they grapple with traumatic events developing from their children. Viewers witness Michelle lying in a hospital bed, needing a heart transplant, while her parents (John and Mary) pray for a miracle. The sequence shortly portrays Maria discussing with her mother (Kate) her desire to go away to college before heading to her car to make food deliveries for her mother's restaurant. Shortly, the screen cuts to Eric walking to his basketball game because his father (David) broke his promise to pick him up on time. The power to reach viewer's hearts is in seeing a disappointed Eric walking down the street with his basketball under one arm, a ringing cell phone in his hand with his father trying to reach him on the way to pick him up, and unaware of distracted Maria approaching him in her car. The scene of the accident portrays how the future of Eric was cut short, Maria's future was altered, and Michelle's was spared because of choices some made and circumstances out of others' control. However, in the end, in the offering of the Newman family's process of healing and forgiveness, the Danielson and Hernandez families experience the gifts of God's forgiveness, grace, mercy, and love that bring about reconciliation and restoration for all three families. *A Question of Faith* provides the opportunity to discern through its cross-cutting parallel storytelling the influence of empathy during life's complexities and unexpected developments that can lead to healing, spiritual growth, and a deeper relationship with Jesus Christ.

Film Analysis: Discerning and Responding to The Message of *A Question of Faith*

The screen story can be a spiritual discipline tool providing spiritual growth as viewers witness how the characters deal with and overcome the adversity that life presents as followers of Jesus Christ. There are layers upon layers of messaging that viewers can discern depending on how their faith is in question at the time of watching *A Question of Faith*. Although questioning one's faith is the overall theme, the subthemes of family relationships, grief, disappointment, racism, purpose, forgiveness, worship, and reconciliation are a few that undergird the overall theme.

In analyzing the film's messages, the screen story offers two opportunities for spiritual growth to viewers actively watching with spiritual discernment. One of the messages communicated in the screen story is the power dynamics of our biological families and the family of Christ. When we, as Christians, learn and live seeing everyone in the Body of Christ as our family members, we will allow more space for love, grace, mercy, forgiveness, and as one of our own. Until we see Christians as honored family members, we will lack the motivation to work toward inclusiveness and equality for those who are different. Our differences span racially, geographically, culturally, and socio-economically but we are bonded through the blood of Christ Jesus.

Christianity transcends the confinements of space, genealogy, genetics, geography, social-economic expectations, racial barriers, and countless other reasons that scrutinize humanity and divide us. Our human connection, which is very complicated, flawed, unreasonable, mysterious, and beautiful, draws us to each other and keeps us together by the grace of God. As the screen story implies, within two hours, work must be intentional to recognize and address how we gracefully love ourselves and our family's dysfunctions. Reconciliation within ourselves, families, and the Body of Christ takes intentional work that may require counsel, therapy, and other resources to address our varying perspectives about people, cultures, and traditions both locally and globally. All the necessary work is not the result of transcendence but the acts of faith we take to do the challenging work of reconciliation. Our works of faith give the Holy Spirit receptive hearts to work with to restore and represent loving, supportive, and Christlike individuals, families, and communities.[15] Witnessing the cross-cutting dynamics in the screen story can demonstrate to viewers how we are bound together, the individual struggles we all experience, and how when one of us is transformed—all who are connected can spiritually grow.

A Question of Faith takes the bonds formed through the family bonded by Christ Jesus and demonstrates the flaws and beauty of our humanness from beginning to end. In between, there are opportunities to see where we are reflected in the characters finding their way through their faith struggles

15. Jas 2:14–26.

to unwavering faith in God's purpose and plan for their lives. Viewers can also see that though we have individual struggles, we are often unaware of how our lives are connected to others we know or may never meet. How we respond in obedience to God and embrace each other can make all the difference that causes a ripple effect that brings glory to God and edifies the whole Body of Christ.

The second message that was present in analyzing the film is reconciliation. In her book, *Roadmap to Reconciliation 2.0: Moving Communities into Unity, Wholeness, and Justice*, Brenda Salter McNeil builds the foundation of understanding with the view that "theology matters" as she leads the practical work of racial reconciliation.[16] She makes an anthropology and sociology connection in claiming that our beliefs about God, people, and communities are interrelated as one informs the other starting with our view of God. As I pull from the theological insights from the previous chapter and lay the theological brickwork for practicing film as a prospective spiritual discipline, I align my foundation in moving forward with Salter McNeil's claim that theology matters in saying that film theology matters. I will highlight a few points she makes on reconciliation and how *A Question of Faith* expresses what she presents in her book, *Roadmap to Reconciliation 2.0: Moving Communities into Unity, Wholeness, and Justice*. She states that there is a lack of agreement on what the term reconciliation means, which poses a problem on how we navigate in going about the ministry of reconciliation.[17] Moving from the perspective of differences in understanding what reconciliation means, she conveys that reconciliation must include repentance, justice, and forgiveness as a Christian.[18] Building from the redemptive story of God, she offers a new definition for reconciliation: "an ongoing spiritual process involving forgiveness, repentance, and justice that restores broken relationships and systems to reflect God's original intention for all creation to flourish."[19] When we consider reconciliation from Salter McNeil's perspective, no matter what our family, church, or community relationship dynamics may be, the work to restore or maintain Christlike relationships is an active and continuous spiritual work that we must engage in intentionally.

---

16. McNeil, *Roadmap to Reconciliation 2.0*, 28–32.
17. McNeil, *Roadmap to Reconciliation 2.0*, 23.
18. McNeil, *Roadmap to Reconciliation 2.0*, 25.
19. McNeil, *Roadmap to Reconciliation 2.0*, 26.

A Question of Faith is an excellent representation of Salter McNeil's definition of reconciliation that leads to restoration. The film takes three culturally diverse families and shows how God loves each one, hears the prayers and cries of everyone who called out in their pain, and answers their prayers in different ways that revealed the purpose of their interconnectedness. Their trauma had the potential to keep them at tremendous odds, but the messages of forgiveness, trust in God, and hope in Christ led to reconciliation. The screen story demonstrates the reconciliation process and what the result can look like when we are intentional in the work of reconciliation. Reconciliation begins with God, cannot be accomplished without God, and is the work of God for us and through us.[20] The actual work of reconciliation is not something we do and never think about again. As Christians, reconciliation is part of our spiritual stories of redemption and how we have been reconciled with God through Jesus Christ. No matter where we find ourselves on the reconciliation journey, we must understand our mission, who we are, where we are going, the plan to get there, and how we will know if we have been successful.[21] Evidence of our success is when we spiritually grow to understand and live out forgiveness, repentance, and expressions of love the way Jesus lived and taught us to follow in his way. There are true stories like the Christian-based biopic film, *I Can Only Imagine* (2018), that demonstrate the power of forgiveness and repentance that leads to healing and transforming love.[22] Our discernment is in acknowledging that through Jesus, we are interconnected, and his influence moves us to transformational relationships.

Soul Surfer (2011)—Biopic

God's Word is clear that our lives will be filled with adversity from the day we are born until we take our last breath. We face circumstances that cause us to stare at a fork in the road and grapple with which way we will go. *Soul Surfer* is a biopic screen story based on the biography, *Soul Surfer: A True Story of Faith, Family, and Fighting to Get Back on the Board* by Bethany Hamilton. A non-fiction Christian-based film functioning as the power of testimony offers a way to impact a person's response towards spiritual growth more likely because the story is true. When considering non-fiction

---

20. McNeil, *Roadmap to Reconciliation 2.0*, 94.
21. McNeil, *Roadmap to Reconciliation 2.0*, 94.
22. Erwin and Erwin, *I Can Only Imagine*.

Christian-based films as a viable spiritual discipline compared to fiction, people may find relating to the real-life account of God's presence in someone's life more influential and tangible.

In the case of this biopic screen story, Bethany is a professional surfer and shares her testimony on how she faced her fears and challenges to move forward after losing her arm in a shark attack. One of the most powerful descriptions of testimony in the Bible is shared in Revelation 12:11, as the Scripture declares that the word of testimony conquers the accuser against our faith. Our adversary accuses us before God, day, and night, but believers have conquered the accuser by the blood of the Lamb and by the word of our testimony.[23] The testimonies (the recounting of our encounters with the Triune God) that we share have the power to make the enemy flee and encourage each other in the faith.

Christian-based biopic films have a more profound capacity for relatability and belief because the story being told is someone's personal account of their relationship with the Triune God. The movies are a creative testimony of how a person has experienced Christ and how they have overcome obstacles to encourage others in their faith. The power of films serve as a testimony of faith to support spiritual growth and deepen a relationship with Jesus Christ by encouraging viewers that if God did it for them, God could do the same for us. With the spiritual insight to discern beyond the screen, *Soul Surfer* presents a real-life tragedy and demonstrates how faith can be challenged, discovered, renewed, and the catalyst to propel us to overcome with hope and into a promised future against all odds.

Film as Storytelling: "A True Story of Faith, Family, and Fighting to Get Back on the Board"[24]

Bethany Hamilton shares the story of how she overcame the loss of her arm due to a shark attack to continue competing in the sport of surfing in the film *Soul Surfer*. Viewers are introduced to Bethany's life by seeing the dynamics of her family with parents who raised their children in the faith of Jesus Christ and to become lovers of surfing. One day while in the water, Bethany is attacked by a shark and loses her left arm. The screen story takes viewers on a one hour and fifty-two-minute capture of how Bethany (AnnaSophia Robb) goes from losing her arm, coming to terms with the fact

---

23. Rev 12:10–11.
24. The title of Bethany Hamilton's book points to her story of faith: *Soul Surfer*.

that she is evidence of a miracle as her life was spared, dealing with the pain of facing the possibility of losing her dream, witnessing how her family stood by her on the journey to healing, and the faith she had in God and herself to fight her way back to the one thing she loved—surfing.

The Apostle Paul speaks of the different seasons of life and how we are able to face and accomplish all things through Christ Jesus.[25] The same Scripture is referenced when Bethany's father (Tom) encourages her as she contemplates continuing in her surfing career. The film offers the opportunity to help viewers witness snapshots of Bethany and her family's faceoff with adversity to see that we can do all things with faith in Christ.

Bethany's testimony shows that during one of the most challenging times in her life, she chose to go on a mission trip with her church's youth group in Thailand, which was recovering from a tsunami. A mission trip to Mexico was originally on her schedule before her accident, but she decided not to go, prioritizing her participation in surfing competitions. Subsequently, her decision played a significant part in the shark attack she experienced because she was at home, surf training.

When Bethany loses her arm, struggles to reclaim an active surfing career, and questions if surfing competing is possible, she decides to go on the Thailand mission to help others and gain perspective on God's plan for her life. While serving those suffering and overcome by fear in Thailand, Bethany is enlightened by love's power over fear. When she returns home to Hawaii, she is flooded with global support from those witnessing her journey to not give up on surfing and discovers how she inspires them to overcome their adversity. All the perspective she gained from getting back on her surfing board and into the ocean, helping others in Thailand, and returning home to discover the inspiration she had become to others, changed her perspective to see God's plan for her life. Bethany chose to remain a surfing athlete, grew in her faith, and became a witness to the power of God in her life. In her transformed perspective, with conviction, she testified that she would not have changed what happened to her because losing her arm allowed her to reach people far beyond what two arms would have allowed her to do.

---

25. Phil 4:11–13.

The Power of Film: The Ministry of Visual Influence

A film's power to take a written story and transform the words into a dramatized reenactment triggers multiple senses for transcendence. Reading Bethany Hamilton's biography impacted those who read the book so much that a movie was made based on her story and demonstrates the power of storytelling. However, the screen story took the experience to another level of empathy. *Soul Surfer*, as a film, penetrated viewers' minds, hearts, and spirits on another sensory level by visually seeing what Bethany endured by visualizing and hearing the reenactment on a screen. The spiritual growth that viewers witness through Bethany's adversity is supported by the camera's vantage points. The camera angles demonstrate the process of her mind being renewed and transformed, leading to a changed perspective. Each frame contributes to the evolution of perspectives, ultimately resulting in her continued pursuit of her life and dreams of becoming a professional surfer. *Soul Surfer* provides an example of how one's perspective can influence what we see or feel about something, someone, or some place. As the movie shares the vantage points of Bethany and those in her life, the camera focuses on specific objects, physical postures, emotional expressions, and spatial depth, to tell the story of each person's perspective. Through the vantage point of a camera filming a particular scene at a specific angle, viewers are persuaded to focus on what the filmmakers intend for us to see and draw us into Bethany's story.

In *Soul Surfer*, the perspective of Bethany is shown by focusing on her love of Jesus, her family, her friends, her community, and surfing. The point of view of her loved ones is also expressed through their support and interactions with Bethany. The plot's sequencing emphasizes body language and expressions of love, joy, and pain to help undergird everyone's responses to Bethany's trauma. The internal conflict that Bethany struggled with in not going on the mission trip to Mexico is expressed from the camera's vantage point as she tries to resolve her guilt in collecting donations. Before Bethany loses her arm, the perspective of the shark targeting her waving arm in the water as she lies on her surfing board is the focus. Simultaneously, the camera captures the shock and panic of her best friend, who witnesses the attack. After adjusting to having one arm and attempting to reclaim her love for surfing, the camera provides the overwhelming process of Bethany falling off the surfboard, getting washed out by the waves, and eventually surrendering to defeat by giving her surfing boards away to adoring fans. The camera's perspective process shows viewers how Bethany's attitude and spirituality were transformed through trauma, disappointment, doubt, fear, and surrender.

As Bethany is challenged to gain a new perspective, viewers visually take the journey with her and those in her life whose attitudes are changing in response to her trauma. A visual expression of Bethany's perspective transformation influences a deeper level of empathy, encouragement, perseverance, and hope in experiencing her process through the camera's vantage point. The filmmakers hone in on the perspective of Bethany and everyone meaningful to her life, including the shark that took her arm. The filmmakers intentionally communicate Bethany's tension in her faith before losing her arm and after. Viewers have a frame of reference of why surfing was like the blood that ran through Bethany's veins by seeing how her entire world was centered around surfing, along with her faith in Jesus Christ. The perspective shared was that her faith in Jesus was not absent from surfing, although there was often a struggle to prioritize the two. The present struggle before her attack was choosing surfing obligations over her ministry commitments. After her accident, the shift in her perspective of prioritizing the two was forced. In losing her arm, Bethany discovered her attitude was challenged, and she had to gain clarity on how she saw herself and life moving forward with her faith in Jesus Christ at the center.

Film Analysis: Discerning and Responding to The Message of *Soul Surfer*

As a potential spiritual discipline, the biographical film (biopic) *Soul Surfer* has many common themes that *A Question of Faith* has in light of how we respond to adversity in our lives. For some seeking to use Christian biopics as a possible spiritual discipline, the more considerable influence that the screen stories may have over Christian fiction is that the life events are actual. *Soul Surfer* is a true story (testimony) shared by Bethany Hamilton, who lived to tell her perspective in the face of adversity. In the story of Bethany Hamilton, her ability to overcome hardship and reclaim her dream of being a professional surfer was in how she envisioned her life through the eyes of faith in Jesus Christ and the community of believers that were her extended circle of family support. Two points to highlight demonstrating spiritual growth that led to a deepened relationship with Jesus Christ for Bethany are 1) having the best perspective and 2) the power of koinonia—"the Christian fellowship or body of believers."[26] The screen story presents Bethany's testimony by showing the tides that turn in her life once she has a positive outlook on her situation and discovers how vital her community has been in the process.

As viewers are introduced to a tight-knit family of faith, there is also insight into how they adjusted to Bethany losing her arm and their journey in supporting her to find her way back to surfing. In the screen story providing snapshots of each family member's response to their loved one being hurt, a subtle picture is painted that nothing we go through in life is happening in a silo of isolated personal pain. As believers, we are all connected, and when one of the members of the Body of Christ hurts, then we all feel pain.[27] There is a common theme between *A Question of Faith* and *Soul Surfer* in how we are connected as family and community. Just as the Hamilton family was bonded by their faith in Jesus Christ, their joy of surfing, and the pureness of joy in the life they lived—they were all tested and had to adjust as their loved one's life was significantly changed. Bethany, her family, and her friend's perspectives were altered by the trauma she had experienced and the necessary changes to live with one arm.

The screen story introduces the theme of perspective through the youth group leader, Sarah (Carrie Underwood). She teaches the youth about the topic of perspective with a scriptural emphasis on Jeremiah 29:11. The Scripture supported Sarah's message by reminding the youth that God knows the plans for their lives, which was not to harm them but to give them a hope and a future.[28] The message would be one that Bethany holds onto during her adversity. After Bethany's accident and her struggle to adjust to living and surfing with one arm; she returns to Sarah to gain an understanding of finding perspective. Sarah ministers to Bethany about perspective, not knowing why something bad happened to her, but believing that God's plan would be revealed in some way. The vulnerability that Bethany shows confiding in and confessing to Sarah has the influence to reach those who struggle with seeking support from others while struggling.

Bethany started with a post-accident attitude that demonstrated that one arm would not keep her from surfing again. Initially, she tells her father (Dennis Quaid) that she does not need her pursuit to surf again to be easy but just possible. Her perseverance was encouraging, but the struggle to do what she envisioned took her to a breaking point that made her choose to give up

26. Merriam-Webster.com Dictionary, "Koinonia."
27. 1 Cor 12:26.
28. Jer 29:11.

her dream. All these things cause her to contemplate her perspective and lead her back to Sarah for guidance. Bethany decides that going to Thailand to help others who have experienced devastation and loss would be purposeful. In her humility in helping others, she was able to empathize with the people and help bring joy back to their lives through the sport she loved—surfing.

After Bethany returned home, her transformed perspective was met by the overwhelming support from letters from around the world, witnessing her get back on her surfing board and try again with one arm. In all these things, Bethany returns to her love of surfing and becomes the professional surfer she had always dreamed of becoming. Viewers witness Bethany's spiritual growth through adversity, gaining perspective, and realizing the good that came out of her traumatic experience. She initially could not see how losing her arm could be a good plan that God had for her, but when her perspective changed, she saw the world open up to her and her message of faith through Jesus Christ. *Soul Surfer* is Bethany's message that has the power to reach the hearts of those who can relate to her traumatic experiences, gain a new perspective, and find hope to persevere.

Through Bethany's expression of doubt, she sought understanding through her faith in Jesus Christ and the community of believers. The presence of koinonia is evident throughout the entire screen story and demonstrates the power of a supportive spiritual community. Witnessing how Bethany's family and friends supported her, as well as how Sarah, her youth group, and the Christian community loved and supported her, is instrumental to spiritual growth. The significance of the fellowship of believers is communicated in Hebrews 10 and continues to be the church's mandate today: "And let us consider how to provoke one another to love and good deeds, not neglecting to meet together, as is the habit of some, but encouraging one another, and all the more as you see the Day approaching."[29]

In a time when the church is experiencing decline, through stories like Bethany's, we can see why koinonia is so essential to the Body of Christ. In itself, churches gathering together in fellowship to watch a film is the expression of community bonding and a corporate spiritual discipline. As a family of believers, we are the iron that sharpens one another to make each other better, and we are to encourage one another as we live a life of faith in Jesus Christ.[30] The screen story sharing a portion of Bethany's life influences viewers to gain perspective and understand why and how our connection as a spiritual community is so vital to persevering in everyday

29. Heb 10:24–25 (NRSVUE).
30. Ps 27:17 and 1 Thess 5:11.

challenges and unimaginable struggles in life. Remembering Bethany's testimony through the vantage point of a camera's lens influences a response to remember what was seen and heard through her story.

Biopic screen stories like *Soul Surfer* have the potential to be a relatable resource to minister to younger generations and seekers in popular culture. Such biopic films can help anyone who engages the genre as a viable spiritual discipline experience spiritual growth. Furthermore, reinforcing what has been seen and heard by contemplating the Scriptures that strengthened Bethany's belief that God had a plan for her life and that she could do all things through Christ can help us spiritually grow and deepen our relationship with Jesus Christ.[31]

Son of God (2014)—Biblically-based

Watching a biblical movie as a possible spiritual discipline is an innovative way to expose the Holy Bible to those who do not read the Word consistently, creatively teach the Word of God, and discuss life issues featured in biblical screen stories. The Holy Bible is the source by which Christians come to know and learn about God, God's relationship with humanity, and God's will for all creation. The Bible is a collection of books that include Scriptures, text, letters, poetry, wisdom writings, and narratives that give a historical account from the beginning of creation to the prophetic revelation of things to come. The story of Jesus' birth, life, death, and resurrection is the in-between within the biblical canon. Christians best know the historical account of Jesus as the Gospels, narrated in the books of Matthew, Mark, Luke, and John. The spiritual disciplines that we practice in spiritual formation as followers of Christ are derived, inspired, and tested against the sacred text of the Holy Bible. As individuals and Christian communities seek to spiritually grow and have a deeper relationship with Jesus Christ, the Holy Bible is the foundational source to teach, guide, correct, and encourage us to do so.

Different biblical interpretations can conflict because of flawed theology. Flawed theology based on subjective interpretation can cause spiritual abuse and troublesome doctrines that can hinder a person's spiritual growth. The spiritual discipline of study with the guidance of the Holy Spirit is crucial to understanding Scripture's context and messaging. Also, we cannot dismiss that, like with any movie, the screen story's portrayal communicates the root of the filmmaker's perspective. With all the cautions considered, the

---

31. Jer 29:11 and Phil 4:11–13.

need for discernment should constantly be reiterated to viewers watching films as a possible spiritual discipline, edutainment, or entertainment.

When a screen story is determined to be biblically-based, filmmakers intend to bring to life the Scriptures, and viewers expect to experience the dramatization of the stories they have read and heard in the Holy Bible. The advice in watching any biblically-based movie is to have the Holy Bible available to understand if the screen story communicates accuracy in how the filmmakers interpret the Scriptures in retelling the stories. There is an awareness of historical gaps in the Holy Bible because the book is an anthology of different texts. Filmmakers must consider how to fill in the gaps through research, other available historical texts, and, when necessary, the imagination. As viewers, we must discern and test what we see and hear so that we are not led away from God's truth communicated in the Scriptures.

Film as Storytelling: A Dramatic Retelling of Sacred Scriptures

The film, *Son of God*, takes the biblical account of the Gospel of John, regarding the synoptic Gospels and the books of Acts and Revelation, to frame the screen story as the Apostle John narrates the story of Jesus from his perspective in the movie. Through the film, viewers witness a dramatization of the Scriptures that tell of Jesus' birth, his time with the disciples, his ministry, crucifixion, resurrection, ascension, and expansion of his teachings through the Apostles. As previously mentioned, the filmmakers take certain liberties to dramatize the text to create cinematic movement. In the case of *Son of God*, I will explore how the creative privileges taken can hinder the film from being used to bring people closer to Jesus by the inaccuracies displayed. However, the film is not necessarily a wasted tool for spiritual growth. The screen story introduces or engages viewers with Jesus' ministry and serves as an example of why we need to study the Scriptures to verify what we have learned about him.

Although the film uses the Holy Bible as a source for its narrative, there are many theological concerns that the movie may warrant for skeptics. Some artistic interpretations will cause Bible scholars and readers to pause to check the accuracy (which I will touch on during my analysis). Viewing the film with the Holy Bible readily available for guidance when used as a tool for spiritual discipline is beneficial. The Bible in hand supports accessing the liberties the filmmakers have taken in portraying the Scriptures that may tell a different story than what the Scriptures communicate.

Incorporating the classical discipline of study when watching biblically-based films, like *Son of God,* complements the ultimate goal of spiritual growth through an edutainment source.

The Power of Film: Discerning and Responding to The Message of *Son of God*

When analyzing *Son of God*, I divert from highlighting two messages the film portrays to examining, more specifically, the potential negative and positive influences biblically-based movies like *Son of God* may have on those engaging them as a possible spiritual discipline. In doing so, I do not deviate from substantiating my central argument claim but acknowledge that God can still use the film for good in some viewers' lives, despite the potential interpretive concerns that may hinder spiritual growth for others. Taking on the stance to view the movie in its "full integrity," *Son of God* offers the opportunity to do so and guides people to be intentionally aware of possible discrepancies when using the genre as a viable spiritual discipline.[32]

I find the approach appropriate for the biblically-based film as Scriptures have a historical foundation of understanding the messages communicated through storytelling. A filmmaker's exegesis and eisegesis of Scripture can open the way to create screen stories that represent the Scriptures based on their motives and interpretations. However, the same motive and interpretation concerns can apply to a preacher's sermon, a teacher's Sunday School lesson, or a small group leader's insight. In all cases, how a filmmaker or church leader portrays the stories of the Holy Bible, accurately or erroneously, may help or run the risk of hindering the process of spiritual growth or deepening a relationship with Jesus Christ. More significantly, filmmakers creating Christian-based screen stories with a Christlike foundation or advisement by Christlike leaders with a theological and spiritual foundation in the Word of God is beneficial.

The Antagonistic Analysis of *Son of God* as a Potential Spiritual Discipline

Although creative space and interpretation are a license given to filmmakers, sometimes pushing the envelope, and going too far will lead some

---

32. Johnston, *Reel Spirituality,* 72.

audiences away from valuing the film's inspirational intentions. *Son of God* does have some interpretive flaws that may cause concern for Bible scholars, theologians, and scripturally aware Christians. There are several instances where altering Scripture is a potential hindrance to spiritual growth or distraction as they take away from the powerful storytelling in the Holy Bible. However, I will record two that missed the opportunity to bring to life the ministry of Jesus that has been read, studied, and preached for centuries that may interfere with one's spiritual development in understanding Jesus' story. I will also use the same two instances to show the possibility of how the film can be a spiritual discipline tool.

The first scene that the filmmakers scripturally alter in the movie, by omitting an important detail, is the story of the woman caught in adultery. The Holy Bible records that the Pharisees accused the woman and tried to trap Jesus (Diogo Morgado) in questioning him concerning her sin. In response to being brought into the situation, Jesus bent down and wrote something on the ground.[33] Though the Scriptures do not reveal what Jesus was writing, the filmmakers omit the action entirely from the film. Instead, the screen story shows Jesus holding up the stone and asking the accusers in the crowd who are without sin.

The filmmakers leave out a significant part of the story and communicate actions contrary to Scripture. Also, the filmmakers passed up a powerful opportunity to demonstrate the visual effects of Jesus, the woman caught in adultery, and the accusers in the crowd. The omitting of Scripture while depicting an alternative story is one concern that could misconstrue one's learning development of the Word of God and having a relationship with Jesus Christ. Such a habit of omitting and adding scripturally inaccurate details can lead to misguidance, distractions, and ammunition to accuse Christians of biasedly sharing what one deems essential from the Bible. In redeeming the scene for spiritual formation, spiritual growth is possible when a viewer can activate and practice the spiritual disciplines of prayer and study in examining screen stories that misrepresent the record of Scripture. The importance of knowing and studying Scripture can be taught and learned as viewers examine such biblical stories with intentional prayer and study.

I recognize the slippery slope in engaging biblically-based films with potentially gross misrepresentations of Scripture in spiritual formation. However, I am also keenly aware that we are not in control of what people

---

33. John 8:1–11.

are watching independently or protect them from the influence of what they watch. With that being said, we must understand and equip believers and seekers on how to navigate, test, and sift what is and is not truth and righteousness. Christlike leaders have a responsibility to equip believers by carrying out the exhortations from the Apostle Paul, "admonish the idlers, encourage the fainthearted, help the weak, be patient with all of them."[34] In doing so, we must consider all forms of temptation and prepare people to overcome them. Referring back to my previous point, it is important to emphasize teaching the recognition of the Holy Spirit's presence and discerning what is good and evil.[35] Whether a novice student of Scripture is motivated to seek clarity or a distinguished scholar is prompted to teach the accuracy of the Scripture, each response to the movie can lead to spiritual growth, which is the goal of a spiritual discipline.

The second scene of inaccuracy is the depiction of how Jesus raised Lazarus from the dead.[36] *Son of God* shows Jesus going into the tomb with Lazarus' body without grave clothes covering him. He says he is the Resurrection and the Life over Lazarus' body before kissing him on the forehead. Lazarus awakes with a gasp of breath and walks out of the tomb. The filmmaker's demonstration of what happened is drastically different from the Scripture. The Gospel of John says that when Jesus arrived in Bethany, he was met by Martha's despair and grief and told her that he was the Resurrection and the Life, and her brother would live again though she misunderstands him. Their alternative view diminishes the power that Jesus displayed in what he said and did and how he said and did those things in performing the miracle of raising Lazarus from the dead.

Before asking about the site of Lazarus' tomb, there are several encounters Jesus has with others that the movie omits. More importantly, according to Scripture, Jesus' prayer and command for Lazarus to come out of his grave were without the gravestone present. Lazarus came out on his own, bound by strips of cloth around his hands, feet, and face. Jesus then told the people to remove the grave clothes and let Lazarus go. In this biblical story, all that Jesus said and did happened outside the tomb of Lazarus. By the filmmakers significantly altering the story told in John 11, the power of Jesus' words was diminished by indicating he was with Lazarus, touching him, and speaking to him in the tomb. There is a theological connection

---

34. 1 Thess 5:14 (NRSVUE).
35. 1 Thess 5:19–21.
36. John 11:1–44.

between God saying, "Let there be," and all of what God spoke was created in the book of Genesis with Jesus, by his word alone, calling Lazarus from the dead.[37] *Son of God* diminishes the influence of its screen story by dramatically changing the biblical account and removing the power of God's Word spoken over our lives. The filmmakers also possibly confuse one's understanding of faith in Jesus, whom we cannot see or touch showing up when we need him. Knowing that Jesus does not have to physically be present to heal, deliver, save, or perform any miracle in our life is crucial to spiritual formation and deepening a faith relationship with Jesus.

I responded to the screen story by opening up my Bible to John 11, even though I knew the account portrayed in the film was inaccurate, to confirm what I knew to be true in the text. In the process, I understood the importance of having spiritual awareness and connection to what the Holy Spirit reveals. The ability to point out how the filmmakers portrayed the details of Jesus raising Lazarus from the dead incorrectly is a result of practicing the spiritual discipline of study. Having the discernment and ability to assess portrayals of biblical accounts and compare them to actual Scripture is the responsibility of believers. We are admonished to, "Do your best to present yourself to God as one approved by him, a worker who has no need to be ashamed, rightly explaining the word of truth."[38] In doing so, I engaged the *Son of God* as a spiritual discipline, undergirded by the classical disciplines.

The practice of both in my spiritual formation helped me spiritually grow in affirming what I knew about Scripture to be true, as I was alerted to the misrepresentation of Scripture, and my convictions about the miraculous power of Jesus Christ. Going a step further, I discovered that The History Channel premiered, *Jesus: His Life*, offering a scripturally accurate retelling of Jesus raising Lazarus from the dead.[39] The 8-episode television series depicts the life, ministry, and resurrection of Christ with scholarly commentary. Using Christian-based films as a viable spiritual discipline with discrepancies like *Son of God*, in the way that I did, can benefit one's spiritual formation and search for the truth of Scripture. Such instances as the two examples I have listed are the pop quizzes that we do not expect that can gauge our spiritual growth and relationship with Jesus Christ.

---

37. Gen 1:1–31.
38. 2 Tim 2:15 (NRSVUE).
39. Pierce et al., *Jesus: His Life*.

The Case for *Son of God* as a Possible Spiritual Discipline

Overall, in examining the screen story, *Son of God*, I conclude that despite inaccurate depictions of some Scripture, the film is a suitable introduction and case study to the life of Jesus Christ and The Gospels. In analyzing the affirming storytelling *Son of God* offers viewers, the film brings to life (through dramatization) the life, ministry, and influence of Jesus Christ. Jesus is seen having a relationship with the people he engaged and how he captured their attention. The ways in which Jesus healed those that were sick are visualized, as well as the responses of those who witnessed the miracles. There are many instances through the dramatization of the Gospel story that can help those who visually learn to comprehend the depth of the Scriptures. The screen story can be used as a possible spiritual discipline to lead people to seek a deeper relationship with Christ by offering visual insight into his life and ministry. The movie also can be a tool for spiritual growth to teach viewers how to grow in discernment and be more intentional in follow-up by studying the Scriptures to test what they have seen and heard in a movie for accuracy.

One must note that though the screen stories offer visual insight, those depictions are interpretations that can be biased and sometimes culturally harmful. Taking into account who is telling the story and why is important in discerning the intention and type of influence the film has on viewers. We should never solely take the preacher's, teacher's, or film's word alone for how we come to know or understand God or the Bible. Each follower of Christ is responsible for studying the Scriptures and accountable for how we learn, work, and live out our faith, rightly dividing the word of truth.[40] In the cases of illiteracy, audio Bibles are helpful tools for studying the Scriptures. However, the acknowledgment is made that films or oral traditions may be the only exposure, as noted by Plantinga in chapter 3, that some communities and cultures have to the Scriptures.

As Christlike leaders, there is another level of responsibility to observe what Christian-based films are exposing to people to guide them through discerning the truth or the misconception of our faith to help in the spiritual growth process and nurturing discernment. Redemption is possible for films such as *Son of God* to be a viable spiritual discipline and a tool to test all things to discern what is true and false according to the Word of God in our spiritual growth.[41]

---

40. 2 Tim 2:15.
41. 1 Thess 5:19–21 (NRSVUE).

Embracing Christian-based Films

One perspective of the story of Jesus that *Son of God* offers that can help viewers grow in understanding is in compiling the different vantage points of the same events shared through Matthew, Mark, Luke, and John. Taking the perspective of the Apostle John from the Gospel of John and Revelation with interwoven accounts of the synoptic Gospels and the book of Acts is a way to present a linear perspective of the story of Jesus. When considering again the weight of different vantage points as outlined in *Soul Surfer*, the Gospels present the points of view from different witnesses to Jesus' life and ministry. The various perspectives are powerful as they witness to the validity of Jesus' story. The ability to put pieces of a puzzle together to create a clearer picture is beneficial in having a greater understanding of the complete story. Using a more linear strategy to create a screen story depicting the life of Jesus removes the scatteredness the Gospels give in communicating different and separate points of view. The filmmakers' innovation takes various teachings of Jesus and places them within scenes where Jesus is actively healing, feeding, and blessing the people with miracles to provide more power to the words with a visual expression of what Jesus was communicating. The New Testament is clear that Jesus was preaching and teaching everywhere he went, using parables as his featured method. Filmmakers take the opportunity to demonstrate Jesus' consistent teaching by merging the Scriptures to complement what Jesus said with what Jesus did. Combining accounts of the same events or encounters can help focus viewers on taking in a comprehensive view of how Jesus was functioning in his life and ministry.

The portrayal of Jesus feeding the multitudes exemplifies *Son of God* merging the Scriptures. All four Gospels tell the story of Jesus taking two fish and five barley loaves of bread from a boy's lunch to feed over 5000 people. The story of Jesus feeding the 5000 is told in Matthew 14:13–21, Mark 6:30–44, Luke 9:10–17, and John 6:1–14. However, the Gospel of John is the only account that mentions the lunch used to feed the multitude belonged to a boy in the crowd. The film only depicts the synoptic Gospels account of the event, which focuses more on Jesus' interaction with the people rather than the testing of the disciples.

In Matthew's account of the story, Jesus had compassion and healed the people. In Mark's version of the event, Jesus began teaching the crowd, while in Luke's version, Jesus healed and taught about the kingdom of God. The filmmakers take the opportunity to add the words from Jesus' Sermon on the Mount found in Matthew 6:25–34 about God's care for the sparrows to demonstrate how God provides much more for humanity. As Luke mentions that Jesus taught the crowds about the kingdom of God in this specific encounter, sharing such teachings from the Sermon on the Mount does not seem to be far-fetched. The Sermon on the Mount and feeding the multitude are not in concordance with one another in the Holy Bible. However, the filmmakers take the words of Jesus' most popular sermon and add them to the feeding of the multitude scene in the screen story to emphasize God's miraculous provision for us.

There is an instance in which *Son of God* demonstrates an incredible visual influence in showing Jesus healing a man of leprosy. The story of Jesus healing the man of leprosy is found in Matthew 8:1–4, Mark 1:40–45, and Luke 5:12–16. The many moments displayed in the screen story, like Jesus feeding the multitude and interacting with and healing the man with leprosy, are the offerings of spiritual growth and nurturing a deeper relationship with Jesus. These types of accounts show how Jesus loved and cared for humanity. The spiritual growth that can occur in witnessing Jesus' interactions comes from learning to do likewise through the spiritual gifts given to us through the Holy Spirit.

Film's power can ignite our senses and demand a response in seeing Jesus touch a man that everyone else was repelled by and who needed healing. Witnessing Jesus unafraid to go near the man shows viewers the love, compassion, and willingness of Jesus to come near us all—no matter our circumstances. Filmmakers using film to bring Scripture to life for seekers and believers in Christ is an effective way to spread the Gospel as Jesus commanded disciples to do. Telling the story of Jesus to demonstrate his love for humanity through his life, death, and resurrection can inspire people to deepen their relationship with Christ and spiritually grow to be transformed by his teachings.

When Jesus tells the story of the Good Samaritan in Luke 10:37, the account records Jesus teaching compassion, "The one who showed him mercy."[42] Jesus said to him, "Go and do likewise."[43] This Scripture is one example of how Jesus expected his followers to do as he had done, as he had taught, and as he had commanded. We are able to do these things because of the power of the Holy Spirit within us as believers, as noted in John 14:26, Luke 24:49, Acts 1:4, and Acts 2:1–13. Additionally, 1 Corinthians 12 explains how the spiritual gifts that believers receive enable us to edify the Body of Christ and disciple others.[44]

---

42. Luke 10:37 (NRSVUE).
43. Luke 10:37 (NRSVUE).
44. Spiritual gifts are also noted in Eph 4:11–16 and Rom 12:4–8.

Again, when considering the power of film engaging multiple senses, *Son of God* is an example of providing viewers with a visual and audible experience of how the Scriptures describe the events in the New Testament. The film does not lose spiritual discipline potential, even though the dramatized attempt has some caution for those new to the Scriptures, not as familiar or easily deterred by contradictions found in the depiction. *Son of God* has the elements of what Jesus describes in the parable of the weeds.[45] There are some good and some bad sown together, but moving too quickly to destroy the weeds found in the film could lead to destroying the good that the film may harvest in spiritual formation.

Profound insight is possible when viewers see Jesus perform a miracle, such as healing a man of leprosy or feeding multitudes with a lunch made for a boy. A greater empathy for Jesus may develop when seeing the gruesome visuals of Jesus whipped, bruised, bloody, nailed to a cross, and dying in agony. Beyond empathy, we have an opportunity to understand the weight of our sins and the price that Jesus paid for humanity to be reconciled to God. Viewers will encounter conservative portrayals of such accounts as the crucifixion and extremist dramatizations. The main focus of my central argument is the ability to discern the truth of each biblical interpretation presented in screen stories and to respond with spiritual growth objectives. Reading or hearing the stories in the Bible causes us to imagine the impossible and the horrific. Such images can potentially have a negative and triggering impact on some viewers that we must consider and address when necessary. However, graphically having those images projected on a screen for us to see is the power of a screen story, potentially penetrating and transforming areas of our hearts previously untouched.

The opportunity to witness someone's life portrayed in a screen story pulls our psyche deeper into an empathetic or sympathetic space that triggers a response. James Merritt had a transcendent and salvific experience by seeing the Scriptures of Jesus' crucifixion come to life for him in a movie theater.[46] The spiritual discernment to look beyond what the screen story is communicating will open the way for the Holy Spirit to move us to a place of spiritual growth. Spiritual growth for Merritt was salvation, which brought him a deeper understanding and relationship with Jesus Christ. *Son of God* influences multiple senses and can move people to at least a better appreciation of Jesus, leading them to a relationship with him even more significantly.

---

45. Matt 13:24–30.
46. Merritt, *52 Weeks with Jesus*, 13–16.

In such biblically-based films like *Son of God*, there may be various responses that are positive and negative. The film may target followers of Christ who can identify altered Scripture in the story or Christians who may not recognize the changes because they have not read or studied the Scriptures consistently with intention. For the sake of viewing such films as a possible spiritual discipline, I return to the advice of Johnston to watch the film in its full integrity. Watching the screen story in its full integrity as a viable spiritual discipline is a surrender to the Holy Spirit's power to lead a viewer to transcendence and transformation. In the process of surrendering to receive the message the Holy Spirit is conveying; we must have faith. Our faith has to move us beyond our biases, theories, theologies, intellect, and any other barrier that interferes with hearing from the Lord. There are times in the Holy Bible when the Spirit of the Lord shows up and asks, "What do you see?" The question is personal, and the Holy Spirit is intentionally working to bring clarity to a message intended for the individual.

Two examples demonstrate that the Holy Spirit works with each individual where they are to see what needs to be seen. The angel of the Lord appeared to Zechariah and asked him, "What do you see?"[47] As the Lord questioned Zechariah even further and he was unable to give an answer, the Lord clarified in verse 6 that understanding would come only by The Lord's Spirit.[48] The Lord continued to reveal what Zechariah needed to know throughout their encounter. The second instance is found in Jeremiah 1:11. The Lord asked Jeremiah, "What do you see, Jeremiah?" In Jeremiah's case, the Lord confirmed that Jeremiah saw correctly (v. 12).[49] The encounters were personal and had two different responses. However, in both cases, God's revelations were made clear to the individuals who needed to understand the message.

Yes, the response can move beyond ourselves and impact those around us. However, Christ deals with us first and our response to the Holy Spirit's question, "What do you see?" is understanding what was told to Zechariah by the angel of the Lord: "Not by might nor by power, but by my Spirit," says the Lord Almighty.[50] Having the ability to discern the screen stories' truth by testing them against Scripture with the Holy Spirit's guidance is a process of spiritual growth. As Christ-like leaders and communities, we have

---

47. Zech 4:2 (NIV).
48. Zech 4:6.
49. Jer 1:11.
50. Zech 4:6 (NIV).

a responsibility to walk alongside those on their personal journey with the Lord. In the case of Christian-based films as a possible spiritual discipline, we are the guardrails that ensure they are not deceived or deterred from their spiritual growth and relationship with Jesus Christ.

CHRISTIAN-BASED FILMS AS A POTENTIAL SPIRITUAL DISCIPLINE EVALUATION

Each of the three films analyzed has the foundational principles of a spiritual discipline. The Gospel of Jesus Christ is present, and the seed of faith is planted as viewers engage in the films as a possible spiritual discipline. The storytelling takes place by introducing, familiarizing, or reaffirming who Jesus is and what a relationship with Jesus Christ looks like for those who seek him. Spiritual growth is demonstrated in each Christian-based genre represented, allowing viewers to see themselves through the stories being told, whether based on actual events, fictional accounts, or historical narratives. Christian-based films as a potential spiritual discipline can "enter the backdoor" of a person's emotions and convey that they are not alone in their suffering, grief, confusion, or uncertainty. Inspiration can be instilled to leave the movie and study the Scriptures, attend a church service or fellowship, or pray that Jesus will come into their hearts and save them from their sins.

In all cases, there are opportunities for viewers to deepen their relationship with Jesus Christ and spiritually grow, which is the purpose of a spiritual discipline. Christian-based films can and do accomplish the goal of a spiritual discipline as the Holy Spirit transforms us. When we encounter a supernatural experience that moves us beyond ourselves, we can discern the Holy Spirit using the movie to speak to our lives and situations. When we can acknowledge we are changed in some way after watching a screen story and are inspired to make changes in our lives, the Holy Spirit has been at work within us. The times we leave a movie to share with others the love of God through Jesus Christ, those are the moments we can trace back to the Holy Spirit as well. Each experience and others not mentioned that are forms of transcendence and transformation is the Holy Spirit helping us to discern beyond the screen to lead us on a journey of spiritual formation and discipleship.

Conclusion

Encountering The Miracle of Spiritual Formation Through Christian-based Films

MIRACLES FROM HEAVEN (2016) is a biopic Christian-based film based on the book written by Christy Beam, bearing its same name.[1] In the screen story, Christy (Jennifer Garner) tells the story of her daughter, Anna (Kylie Rogers), who battled with a chronic and incurable gastroenterological disease and how a near-death experience after falling through the center of a hollowed-out cotton tree in their yard miraculously saved her life. There are many similar themes of faith struggles and how adversity challenges a family in *Miracles from Heaven*, also seen in the fiction film, *A Question of Faith*. Also, similar subjects of wrestling with God's plan through suffering and the power of koinonia seen in the biopic, *Soul Surfer*, are present as Christy and her husband, Kevin (Martin Henderson), lead their family through the adversity in public as a result of their daughter's suffering. The movie adds another subject of faith that we wrestle with as believers and non-believers in believing in God's miraculous power. As Christy shared how Anna was a living testimony to God's miraculous power and people questioned the validity of her testimony, their lack of faith did not nullify the miracle God performed in their lives.

Ultimately, all that I have presented in substantiating my claim that Christian-based films can be a viable spiritual discipline for spiritual formation rests on our faith and actions. Suppose we intentionally do the work and believe that the Holy Spirit can miraculously lead us to a transcendent and transforming experience. In that case, we may spiritually grow and develop a more profound relationship with Jesus Christ while becoming

---

1. Riggin, *Miracles from Heaven*.

CONCLUSION

witnesses to the power of sacramental imagination. Whether other people around us believe or not in the miraculous spiritual discipline work that the Holy Spirit has done in us through screen stories does not invalidate the truth of our transformative experiences. God does not exist and work with constraints as we do as human beings. Therefore, the miraculous transcendence and transformation that we may experience in such ordinary experiences as watching a movie are not impossible with God.[2]

In examining *Miracles from Heaven*, there is a scene where Christy's pastor calls her to meet with him at church. Reverend Scott (John Carroll Lynch) reached out to Christy to discuss why she has not returned to church since being consumed by Anna's illness. She initially explained that staying away was because of interactions with some insensitive members of the congregation in the community. Reverend Scott discerns the actual root cause and leads her to a discussion that reveals the truth of her church absence, which is Christy's disappointment with God. As Christy shares her doubts concerning God's love, Reverend Scott shares with her that during the lowest moments in his life, he tried living doing all he could to connect with God, and he tried to live by walking away from God. The revelation that he discovered through both experiences is that one felt much better than the other.

Reverend Scott's wisdom shared with Christy resonated with me and brought me to a conclusion that are among my final thoughts concerning my central argument claim. I have concluded that we can continue ignoring that Christian-based films can be a viable spiritual discipline and miss the opportunity to reach people through screen stories. Or, intentionally, pay attention to how encountering Christian-based films as a possible spiritual discipline in spiritual formation can lead to spiritual growth and a deepened relationship with Jesus Christ. In alignment with the sentiments of Reverend Scott, I have carefully considered both options to substantiate my central argument. One option stands out to me as superior: intentionally utilizing Christian-based films as an innovative resource to reach the hearts of God's people and guide them toward spiritual growth as a spiritual discipline.

INFLUENCING SPIRITUAL FORMATION THROUGH CHRISTIAN-BASED FILMS

When observing the history and evolution of storytelling and Christians' roles in filmmaking, there is much criticism around the quality and theology

2. Luke 1:37.

of Christian-based film productions. However, independent production of Christian-based films gives way to sharing the messages that they believe God has commissioned followers of Christ to spread throughout the world. Also, providing resourceful content supports using Christian-based films as a viable spiritual discipline to nurture spiritual growth and deepen a relationship with Jesus Christ. As assessment and criticism will continue to take place surrounding the quality, theology, and biases of most Christian-based films, the hope is that the growing subgenre of filmmaking will continue to improve as cinema has done since the late 1800s. In the meantime, Christian-based films have the power to speak to people's hearts through their storytelling mechanism to glorify God and edify the people of God in Jesus Christ. Discerning beyond all the reasons that one may have contrary to Christian-based films may give us the eyes to see and the ears to hear what the Holy Spirit is revealing to us from the heart of God. This revelation allows us to have life more abundantly through Christ Jesus.[3]

The world we live in is constantly changing, and screen stories have been a means that God can use to bring clarity to our lives. Spiritual formation is a personal journey and a corporate experience we share together as the Body of Christ. Whether we seek spiritual formation in our own respective faith walk or the space of koinonia, becoming more Christlike is the goal. In either case, the spiritual disciplines are the exercises we need to engage with consistency to help initiate, establish, grow, and sustain a relationship with Jesus Christ. When developing a spiritual growth plan, no one size fits all exists. Yes, there are foundational principles that we build upon, such as the classical spiritual disciplines. I also acknowledge that Jesus has given us a blueprint for the foundation that guides us in building upon all he has taught us as followers. Jesus speaks about being hearers and doers in response to his teachings. Those who heard and acted wisely were likened to those who built their house on a rock instead of sinking sand.[4]

Following the blueprint and building upon the foundation of spiritual disciplines, including Christian-based films as a viable spiritual discipline, has the spiritual weight to nurture spiritual growth and prosper the souls of those who use the genre in spiritual formation. Christlike individuals and leaders who discern how God is using Christian-based films as the evolution method of storytelling that Jesus mastered have recognized the

---

3. John 10:10.
4. Matt 7:24–29.

Conclusion

greater works that Jesus said his disciples would be able to do with the help of the Holy Spirit.[5]

Dallas Willard is clear that spiritual formation work is not possible without the working of the Holy Spirit within us, and he also acknowledges that not all spiritual formation work is by the Holy Spirit.[6] Not every spiritual encounter or practice is a prompting or result of the Holy Spirit's influence. His distinguishing of the spiritual formation work is crucial when considering screen stories as a possible spiritual discipline. I claim that Christian-based films as a potential spiritual discipline must be more than "sitting before a screen searching" because we will always find something spiritual to identify with or become opposed to in the search. Proceeding to engage in the spiritual formation work with intention, discernment, and surrendering to the Holy Spirit working within us is the search for a divine encounter and transformation.

Readdressing Willard's thoughts on spiritual formation he says, "We have to recognize that spiritual formation in us is something that is also done to us by those around us, by ourselves, and by activities which we voluntarily undertake."[7] Considering Willard's point, we must intentionally open ourselves up to engage in spiritual formation and do the necessary spiritual work to surrender to the Holy Spirit's work being done through Christian-based films. In other words, when we practice the spiritual disciplines, engage with other followers of Christ, and seek ways to be spiritually formed into the likeness of Christ, we give way for the Holy Spirit to do the work of transforming us into being Christlike. As a movie viewer, all of the previous entities can be present in the moment as we gather together to watch screen stories as the Body of Christ, just as we often do for Sunday worship each week. The aesthetics may differ; however, the spiritual atmosphere can be just as powerful and give way to long-lasting transformative memories.

We are responsible for doing the work as Willard advised in our spiritual discipline practice. Again, reminding us that spiritual disciplines are the exercises or activities that enable us to receive more of Christ and his power without harming ourselves or others.[8] If a Christian-based film does no harm and helps a person or group to embrace more of Christ and his influence, then adding the practice to the list of spiritual disciplines is

---

5. John 14:12–26. See Higgins, *How Movies Helped Saved My Soul*, 255.
6. Willard, "Spiritual Formation," para 46.
7. Willard, "Spiritual Formation," para 45.
8. Willard, *Spirit of the Disciplines*, 156.

discerning and advocating a storytelling method God is using to reach the hearts of people.

When I was engaging in various fitness challenges during the initial months of the global pandemic in 2020, virtually with a group of friends, there were several areas of my body I wanted to get stronger. Each of us decided what we needed as individuals to maintain a fitness regimen. We would then gather together each week to share our progress, offer suggestions, and encourage each other in our fitness plans. However, we were each responsible for being disciplined in the necessary work to reach our goals. I determined that planks, stretching, squats, and weight-lifting exercises would be my best options. I was deeply intimidated by some of the activities, even though I knew that each workout transformed my body into what I had envisioned to be healthier and more robust. As I engaged in each challenge for the time suggested, I began to experience the results. Not only did I witness my body transforming in shape, but also my endurance increased over time. Moreover, I had formed a routine that the exercises naturally became integrated into my lifestyle. I allowed myself the grace to grow and received the gift of physical, mental, and emotional transformation. I imagine incorporating Christian-based films as a viable spiritual discipline into the spiritual formation category is like my fitness challenges.

If you are a visual person like I am, there is the imagery of muscles getting stronger and stronger with each movement every time there is physical activity. We have to decide to begin the process and choose what will work best for our spiritual training. Not everyone is interested in planks and may opt for sit-ups. In the same vein, watching screen stories may be the spiritual discipline exercises that some need and work effectively for their spiritual growth. The onset of viewing Christian-based films as a possible spiritual discipline may be intimidating, awkward, or even impossible for some. My discerning perspective advises that the more we equip ourselves with how to best facilitate the practice of Christian-based films as a potential spiritual discipline, the more resources we have in our spiritual toolbelt to become more spiritually mature. The Holy Spirit will meet us in our efforts, and we will experience the growth in grace resulting in the gift of spiritual transformation.

Conclusion

CHRISTIAN-BASED FILMS SPIRITUALLY FORMING AND DISCIPLING THE CHURCH AND COMMUNITY

Just as some of us struggle to keep a physical exercise routine to maintain our overall health, others also find keeping a spiritually healthy schedule of practicing the spiritual disciplines for our ultimate well-being. More times than I can count, I have witnessed followers of Jesus Christ share their challenges in keeping a spiritual discipline regimen. Regrettably, some among the count are unaware of spiritual disciplines or how to engage in spiritual formation. Among the people struggling with a healthy spiritual discipline practice are pastoral leaders and laypeople. We must take notice and incorporate the resources that will guide them and inspire people to desire to integrate spiritual discipline practices within their daily lives. As we may have heard the adage repeatedly throughout life, "practice makes perfect." Like anything in life, if we expect to experience success, we must be intentional and consistent with achieving fruitful results. When we discover the spiritual practices that fuel our passion for spiritual growth, work best for us, and align with the principles of Jesus Christ, we will begin to see the results we seek to obtain.

Films have spiritually influenced people like James Merritt, Gareth Higgins, Carl Plantinga, Robert K. Johnston, Craig Detweiler, Kutter Callaway, others shared throughout this book, and myself. In addition, how many countless movie viewers worldwide are watching screen stories and, more likely than not, are having experiences of spiritual transcendence, transformation, and growth and do not know how to process the experience beyond the moment? What resources or leadership are in place to help guide them through the spiritual journey a film may help them process life spiritually, theologically, psychologically, and culturally? As Christlike leaders and disciples of Jesus Christ, who believe, live, and teach what he taught, we must acknowledge how God has continuously worked outside our relentlessly created constraints. Once we do, we seek to learn how to open ourselves to sacramental imagination, personally experience spiritual growth, and become equipped to help others do the same.

As the Body of Christ, we need to move outside the constraints we continue to construct. We should consider the Christian social innovation flourishing concept that L. Gregory Jones introduces and apply the thought to spiritual formation as discussed in chapter 3.[9] Jones makes a poignant

---

9. Jones, *Christian Social Innovation*, 2–3.

point that supports my claim that Christian-based films should be considered viable spiritual disciplines to help people grow spiritually and seek a deeper relationship with Jesus Christ. I reiterate Jones' point that there are too many complex, wicked, complicated, and hard challenges that we face in the world to have a linear approach to addressing them all.[10] I am saying, in conclusion, that people are facing so many unimaginable challenges and new-age concepts shifting and keeping many of them away from the Triune God, church, and anything that has to do with Christianity. As Christians continue fulfilling Jesus' Great Commission mandate, we must continue to find innovative approaches to share the Gospel and nurture the spiritual growth of believers and followers of Jesus Christ.

Psalm 24:1 says, "The earth is the Lord's, and everything in it. The world and all its people belong to him."[11] Movies are not an exclusion from the list of things that belong to God, nor are the people who enjoy watching them. The genre has lasted longer than most have lived and appears to be going strong enough to last well beyond what most of us will exist to be. Cinema has been around for over a century. In knowing film's history, the truth is that Christians have utilized the invention for ministry since the early 1900s. Christian-based films are not a new concept, and using the subgenre to nurture spiritual growth is present in the historical collaboration between Herbert Booth and Joseph Perry.[12] As the evolution of Christian-based film has presented new opportunities for ministry for our generation and the generations to come, we have the responsibility to discern innovative ways to utilize the visual storytelling method for spiritual formation and to engage discipleship in our communities.

Popular culture watches movies daily, whether in movie theaters, community venues, or by streaming them on their personal devices. The core idea of this book is to present an innovative approach to incorporate Christian-based films as a potential spiritual discipline to facilitate spiritual formation. The objective is to help believers in Jesus Christ grow closer to him and in their Christian faith by using a well-liked means of entertainment. Also, going a step further in acknowledging how the results of doing so can equip believers for discipleship through watching movies. My proposal to initiate Christian-based films into the spiritual discipline category of spiritual formation recognizes the influence screen stories already

---

10. Jones, *Christian Social Innovation*, 1.
11. Ps 24:1 (NLT).
12. Johnston, *Reel Spirituality*, 32.

CONCLUSION

have on society that ultimately demand a response to what we have viewed. Suppose we approach our viewership with intention and surrender to the Holy Spirit's guidance. In that case, we can discern beyond the screen and respond by using Christian-based films as a viable spiritual discipline in our spiritual formation. Doing so postures us to have the eyes to see and the ears to hear the messages that Jesus Christ speaks to our hearts to draw us closer to him and take us on a spiritual growth journey through the creative imagination of screen stories. Ultimately, witnessing God's miraculous work through the power of cinema with transcendence, transformation, and spiritual formation in people's lives as a result.

Appendix

CHRISTIAN AND FAITH-BASED FILM VIEWING RESOURCES AND WEBSITES

THE FOLLOWING LIST COMPRISES Christian and faith-based film production companies, streaming accessible websites, and websites that provide Christian-based viewing resources. The list is not comprehensive, nor do I give the information to endorse the companies or content that the websites display. The list provides a starting point for those who seek to explore Christian-based films that are available to pursue the objective of this book.

- *A Conversation with Martin Scorsese on Faith and Film*, Fuller Seminary Fuller Studio, Jan 31, 2017. YouTube.com, https://youtu.be/_w6bIgcgCOc.
- Affirm Films: https://www.affirmfilms.com/ and https://www.affirmfilms.com/discussion-guides/
- Angel Studios, https://www.angel.com/
- Big Idea Entertainment: https://www.veggietales.com/
- ChristianCinema.com: https://www.christiancinema.com/digital/
- Cloud Ten Pictures: https://www.cloudtenpictures.com/
- Conversation Spaces | Michelle Lang-Raymond—"The Arts are a Divine Gift from God," Fuller Studios, Oct 5, 2021, YouTube.com, https://www.youtube.com/watch?v=rAQGYS6IDeU.
- *Exclusive: Martin Scorsese discusses his faith, his struggles, and "Silence,"* America—The Jesuit Review, Dec 8, 2016, YouTube.com, https://youtu.be/TbYiGdinejU.

Appendix

- *Films with a message of faith*, YouTube.com, Apr 21, 2019, https://www.youtube.com/watch?v=RGawDXDCVGQ&list=WL&index=55.
- Five & Two Pictures: https://www.fiveandtwopictures.com/
- Fox Faith: https://www.fishflix.com/collections/fox-faith
- Franklin Entertainment: https://devonfranklin.com/entertainment/
- Fuller Seminary Fuller Studio, https://fullerstudio.fuller.edu/.
- Kendrick Brothers: https://kendrickbrothers.com/
- Kingdom Story Company: https://www.kingdomstorycompany.com/
- Lightworkers Media: https://lightworkers.com/
- On the 7 with Dr. Sean. "Holly Carter Talks Faith-Based Entertainment & Working With Usher—On The 7 With Dr. Sean." FOX Soul, Jan 18, 2020. YouTube.com, https://youtu.be/zieMUPqYjq4, (11:18—14:25)
- Pauline Center for Media Studies: https://media.pauline.org
- Provident Films: https://www.providentfilms.org/
- Pure Flix Entertainment: https://www.pureflix.com/
- Relevé Entertainment: http://releve-ent.com/
- Reverence Gospel Media: http://www.rgmusa.com/
- Sherwood Pictures: https://sherwoodbaptist.net/ministries/sherwood-pictures/
- TD Jakes Enterprises: https://www.tdjakes.com/entertainment/
- That Sister: https://www.thatsister.com/black-christian-Movies/
- Trinity Broadcasting Network: https://watch.tbn.org/p/oyL7iSRi
- UP Faith and Family: https://my.upfaithandfamily.com/black-film-and-tv
- World Wide Pictures: https://billygraham.org/tv-and-radio/worldwide-pictures/

Appendix

CHRISTIAN AND FAITH-BASED FILMS LIST [1]

1. Gods at War (2012–)
2. AHA (2014–)
3. Modern Day Miracles (2017)
4. Bobbi Jo: Under the Influence (2021)
5. Jesus of Nazareth (1977)
6. One: The Woodlawn Study (2016–)
7. A Charlie Brown Christmas (1965 TV Movie)
8. The Last Reformation: The Beginning (2016)
9. Ben-Hur (1959)
10. When Calls the Heart (2014)
11. Life Changes Everything: Discover Zac Ryan (2017)
12. Undaunted . . . The Early Life of Josh McDowell (2011)
13. Free Burma Rangers (2020)
14. The Man from Earth (2007)
15. Chasing After You (2019)
16. The Testaments: Of One Fold and One Shepherd (2000)
17. The Ten Commandments (1956)
18. Dolly Parton's Coat of Many Colors (2015 TV MOVIE)
19. Prophecies of the Passion (2005 TV MOVIE)
20. Elmer Gantry (1960)
21. Mass (2021)
22. The Insanity of God (2016)
23. Gifted Hands: The Ben Carson Story (2009 TV MOVIE)
24. The Insult (2017)

---

1. The list of Christian Movies provided is comprised of 320 films classified as "Christian" or "Faith-based" Movies (as of April 22, 2024). See "300 Christian Movies," www.FitForFaith.ca by fitforfaith-ministries, created—25 Feb 2019, and also https://www.imdb.com/list/ls046089776/?st_dt=&mode=simple&page=1&ref_=ttls_vw_smp&sort=list_order,asc, accessed March 19, 2023. I have contributed additional films to the list beginning at 321–46.

Appendix

25. H2O: A Journey of Faith (2006)
26. The Gospel of John (2003)
27. The Three Wise Men (2006)
28. Acts of God (2014)
29. Les Misérables (2012)
30. Marjoe (1972)
31. The Blind Side (2009)
32. The Hiding Place (1975)
33. Sabina: Tortured for Christ—The Nazi Years (2021)
34. The Last Temptation of Christ (1988)
35. Tyrannosaur (2011)
36. 1 Message (2011)
37. Dead Man Walking (1995)
38. Jesus of Montreal (1989)
39. So, Who Is This Jesus? (1999 TV Movie)
40. The Bible (2013)
41. Where Is My Home (2017)
42. A.D. The Bible Continues (2015)
43. A Walk to Remember (2002)
44. Billy Graham: An Extraordinary Journey (2018 TV Movie)
45. Not a Fan (2010–)
46. Jesus Christ Superstar (1973)
47. Tender Mercies (1983)
48. I Can Only Imagine (2018)
49. Lorenzo's Oil (1992)
50. Behind the Sun (1995 Video)
51. Against the Tide: Finding God in an Age of Science (2020)
52. The Ultimate Gift (2006)
53. Love Comes Softly (2003 TV Movie)
54. The Selfish Giant (2013)

Appendix

55. Tortured for Christ (2018)
56. The Visual Bible: Acts (1994)
57. The Red Tent (2014)
58. Nefarious: Merchant of Souls (2011)
59. Chariots of Fire (1981)
60. Revelation: The Bride, the Beast & Babylon (2013)
61. A Return to Grace: Luther's Life and Legacy (2017)
62. The Passion of the Christ (2004)
63. Kingdom of Heaven (2005)
64. The Patriot (2000)
65. Agora (2009)
66. The Physician (2013)
67. The Apostle (1997)
68. Of Gods and Men (2010)
69. The Easter Experience (2007–)
70. Mountain Top (2017)
71. Unconditional (IV) (2012)
72. Patterns of Evidence: Exodus (2014)
73. Something to Sing About (2000 TV Movie)
74. The Final Prophecies (2010 Video)
75. The Prince of Egypt (1998)
76. The Jesus Film (1979)
77. Procession (2021)
78. Beyond the Next Mountain (1987)
79. MidRange (2013)
80. The Crossing (1994)
81. King of Kings (1961)
82. Soul Surfer (2011)
83. Searching for a King: Israel's United Kingdom (2019)
84. Trial & Triumph: Revelation's Churches (2021)

Appendix

85. Courageous (I) (2011)
86. The Jesus Music (2021)
87. The Merchant of Venice (2004)
88. The Last Champion (2020)
89. The Miracle Maker (2000)
90. Like Dandelion Dust (2009)
91. Clancy (2009)
92. The God Who Speaks (2018)
93. The Perfect Gift (2009)
94. The Sereer: Desperately Trying to Please God (2014)
95. Patterns of Evidence: The Red Sea Miracle (2020)
96. The Creation (1988)
97. Hudson Taylor (1981)
98. Barabbas (1961)
99. Love Takes Wing (2009 TV Movie)
100. To Save a Life (2009)
101. Jesus: Countdown to Calvary (2018 TV Movie)
102. Nine Days (2020)
103. Pieces of Easter (2013)
104. Restored Me (2016)
105. The Case for Heaven (2022)
106. Cry from the Mountain (1985)
107. Badge of Faith (2015)
108. Come the Morning (1993)
109. The Printing (1990)
110. Christmas Oranges (2012)
111. Youth of Christ (2011)
112. It's a Life Worth Living (2020)
113. The Encounter (I) (2010)
114. The Nativity Story (2006)

Appendix

115. End of the Spear (2005)
116. The Gospel of Luke (2015)
117. Snow Angels (I) (2007)
118. Apostle Peter and the Last Supper (2012)
119. Billy: The Early Years (2008)
120. The Woodcarver (2012)
121. Have a Little Faith (2011 TV Movie)
122. Seasons of Gray (2013)
123. The American Bible Challenge (2012–)
124. As I Stand (2013)
125. God of Wonders (2008 Video)
126. The Soloist (2009)
127. When the Game Stands Tall (2014)
128. Time to Run (1973)
129. The Story of Ruth (1960)
130. Victor (II) (2015)
131. Flywheel (2003)
132. October Baby (2011)
133. Faith Like Potatoes (2006)
134. China Cry: A True Story (1990)
135. The Secrets of Jonathan Sperry (2008)
136. Uncle Nino (2003)
137. Patterns of Evidence: Journey to Mount Sinai (2022)
138. The Perfect Stranger (2005)
139. Patterns of Evidence: Moses Controversy (2019)
140. Virtuous (2015)
141. Bamboo in Winter (1991)
142. I Still Believe (2020)
143. The Greatest Story Ever Told (1965)
144. For Pete's Sake! (1966)

Appendix

145. Paul, Apostle of Christ (2018)
146. Same Kind of Different as Me (2017)
147. Facing the Giants (2006)
148. Outlaws (2012)
149. Charge Over You (2010)
150. Twist of Fate (2013 TV Movie)
151. Miracle Maker (II) (2015)
152. Amazing Love (2012)
153. Another Perfect Stranger (2007)
154. The Emissary: A Biblical Epic (1997)
155. Beware of Christians (2011)
156. Stephen's Test of Faith (1998 Video)
157. Where Hope Grows (2014)
158. Leaving Limbo (2013)
159. Overcomer (2019)
160. War Room (2015)
161. Godspell (1973)
162. Joseph: King of Dreams (2000 Video)
163. Fireproof (2008)
164. Woodlawn (2015)
165. Luther (2003)
166. The Bible Collection: Esther (1999 TV Movie)
167. Jonah: A VeggieTales Movie (2002)
168. Nocturnal Agony (2011)
169. Thin Ice (1988)
170. The Grace Card (2010)
171. King's Faith (2013)
172. Brother John (1971)
173. Ring the Bell (2013)
174. Tyson's Run (2022)

Appendix

175. Caught (1987)
176. Love Different (2016)
177. Dialtone (2009 Video)
178. Risen (2016)
179. Evolution's Achilles' Heels (2014)
180. Like Arrows (2018)
181. Until Forever (2016)
182. The Case for Christ (2017)
183. The Star (2017)
184. The Christmas Candle (2013)
185. Because of Grácia (2017)
186. Pilgrim's Progress (2008)
187. Pilgrim's Progress (2019)
188. The Lost & Found Family (2009)
189. Late One Night (2001)
190. Breakthrough (2019)
191. One Night with the King (2006)
192. Do You Believe? (2015)
193. The Resurrection of Gavin Stone (2017)
194. Grace Unplugged (2013)
195. Priceless (II) (2016)
196. Not Easily Broken (2009)
197. The Book of Daniel (2013)
198. The Encounter: Paradise Lost (2012)
199. Saving Sarah Cain (2007)
200. Midnight Clear (2006)
201. Lifemark (2022)
202. Hope Bridge (2015)
203. Stand Strong (2011)
204. Milltown Pride (2011)

Appendix

205. Touched by an Angel (1994–2003)
206. Seven Days in Utopia (2011)
207. God's Compass (2016)
208. The Song (I) (2014)
209. Slamma Jamma (2017)
210. Touched by Grace (2014)
211. The Genius Club (2006)
212. Run the Race (2018)
213. I'm Not Ashamed (2016)
214. Come Sunday (2018)
215. Foundations (2021)
216. Blue Like Jazz (2012)
217. Home Run (2013)
218. Remember the Goal (2016)
219. The Climb (2002)
220. No Greater Love (2010)
221. The Holy Roller (2010)
222. Unplanned (I) (2019)
223. The Master Designer: The Song (2014)
224. Son of God (2014)
225. An Interview with God (2018)
226. A Question of Faith (2017)
227. Joyful Noise (2012)
228. Hoovey (2015)
229. Unbroken: Path to Redemption (2018)
230. Indivisible (II) (2018)
231. A Week Away (2021)
232. Not Today (2013)
233. The Young Messiah (2016)
234. The Cross (2009)

Appendix

235. Catching Hearts (2012)
236. Last Days in the Desert (2015)
237. For the Glory (2012)
238. I Am Michael (2015)
239. Beautifully Broken (2018)
240. This Is Our Time (2013)
241. Polycarp (2015)
242. Nowhere Safe (2014 TV Movie)
243. Faith Happens (2006)
244. Mary, Mother of Jesus (1999 TV Movie)
245. I Am... Gabriel (2012 Video)
246. Last Flight Out (2004)
247. The Pardon (2013)
248. Invisible Enemies (1997 Video)
249. The Homecoming (1996)
250. God Bless the Broken Road (2018)
251. Captive (II) (2015)
252. The Trail (2013)
253. Born to Win (2014)
254. Reconciliation (2009)
255. A Cowgirl's Story (2017)
256. Blessed and Cursed (2010)
257. Sarah's Choice (2009 Video)
258. Mercy Streets (2000)
259. The River Within (2009)
260. Come What May (I) (2009)
261. Never Heard (2018)
262. Wildflower (II) (2014)
263. Time Changer (2002)
264. The Book of Ruth: Journey of Faith (2009 Video)

Appendix

265. Old Fashioned (2014)
266. The Identical (2014)
267. Preacher's Kid (2010)
268. Genesis: Paradise Lost (2017)
269. Break Every Chain (2021)
270. Open My Eyes (2014)
271. Palau the Movie (2019)
272. Between Heaven and Ground Zero (2012)
273. The Girl Who Believes in Miracles (2021)
274. The Mircale of the Cards (2001 TV Movie)
275. Power Play (1994)
276. I Believe (2017)
277. Gallows Road (2015)
278. Beyond the Mask (2015)
279. Tribulation (2000)
280. Believe Me (2014)
281. The Moment After II: The Awakening (2006)
282. The Coming Convergence (2017)
283. The Ark (2015 TV Movie)
284. The Fight Within (2016)
285. The Gospel (2005)
286. Secret of the Cave (2006)
287. The Imposter (2008)
288. Aimee Semple McPherson (2006)
289. Princess Cut (2015)
290. Holyman Undercover (2010)
291. Kirk Cameron: Connect (II) (2018)
292. A Wise Fool (2015 TV Movie)
293. WWJD What Would Jesus Do? The Journey Continues (2015)
294. God's Not Dead (2014)

Appendix

295. The Healing (1983 Video)
296. Lay It Down (2001)
297. The Masked Saint (2016)
298. God's Not Dead: A Light in Darkness (2018)
299. Wild Faith (2018)
300. Alone Yet Not Alone (2013)
301. Samson (2018)
302. I'm in Love with a Church Girl (2013)
303. The Remaining (I) (2014)
304. God's Not Dead 2 (2016)
305. My Daddy's in Heaven (2017)
306. Unstoppable (2013)
307. Christian Mingle (2014)
308. The Widow's Might (2009)
309. Jerusalem Countdown (2011)
310. Let the Lion Roar (2014)
311. Second Glance (1992)
312. Me & You, Us, Forever (2008)
313. The Mark (I) (2012)
314. Last Ounce of Courage (2012)
315. A Matter of Faith (2014)
316. Persecuted (I) (2014)
317. The UnMiracle (2017)
318. Unidentified (2006)
319. The Atheist Delusion (2016 Video)
320. Nothing to Lose (2018)
321. Father Stu (2022)
322. Dog Gone (2023)
323. Rescued by Ruby (2022)
324. The Man of God (2022)

Appendix

325. The Wait (2021)
326. Blue Miracle (2021)
327. Walk. Ride. Rodeo (2019)
328. God Calling (2018)
329. Nothing to Lose 2 (2019)
330. The Clark Sisters: The First Ladies of Gospel (2020 TV Movie)
331. Black Nativity (2013)
332. Woman Thou Art Loosed (2012)
333. Faith Under Fire (2018)
334. Highway to Heaven (2021)
335. Seven Deadly Sins Anthology (2021–2023)
336. My Brother's Keeper (2020)
337. No Vacancy (2022)
338. Family Camp (2022)
339. Jesus Revolution (2023)
340. On a Wing and a Prayer (2023)
341. Ordinary Angels (2024)
342. Cabrini (2024)
343. Unsung Hero (2024)
344. Sound of Hope: The Story of Possum Trot (2024)
345. The Forge (2024)
346. Bonhoeffer (2024)

Bibliography

"300 Christian Movies." by fitforfaith-ministries, 25 Feb 2019. https://www.imdb.com/list/ls046089776/?st_dt=&mode=simple&page=1&ref_=ttls_vw_smp&sort=list_order,asc.

Barber, Andrew. "The Problem with Christian Films." The Gospel Coalition, August 18, 2014. https://www.thegospelcoalition.org/article/the-problem-with-christian-films/.

Berkman, John, and Michael Cartwright, eds. *The Hauerwas Reader*. Durham: Duke University Press, 2001.

Bible Love Notes. "5 Lies About God's Character Promoted in 'The Shack'—Scripture vs. Shack." https://biblelovenotes.blogspot.com/2009/02/5-lies-about-gods-character-promoted-in.html.

Biblegateway.com Encyclopedia of the Bible. "Parable." https://www.biblegateway.com/resources/encyclopedia-of-the-bible/Parable.

———. "Parable." https://www.britannica.com/topic/mashal.

Black, Stacey K., dir. *Highway to Heaven*. A&E Television Networks, 2021. 1 hr. 27 min.

Bradshaw, Peter. "The Shack Review: a wet weekend at Christian Disneyland." *The Guardian*, June 8, 2017. https://www.theguardian.com/film/2017/jun/08/the-shack-review-christian-murder-drama-theology.

Bugbee, Bruce. *Discover Your Spiritual Gifts the Network Way: 4 Assessments for Determining Your Spiritual Gifts: Zondervan*, 2005.

———, and Don Cousins. *Network Participant's Guide: The Right People, in the Right Places, for the Right Reasons, at the Right Time*. Grand Rapids: Zondervan, 2005.

Carnegie, Dale. *How to Win Friends & Influence People: The Only Book You Need to Lead You to Success*. Rev. ed. New York: Gallery, 1998.

Chandler, Diana. "'The Shack' film stirs debate as did preceding book." Baptist Press, February 27, 2017. https://www.baptistpress.com/resource-library/news/the-shack-film-stirs-debate-as-did-preceding-book/.

Chang, Justin. "A Christian critic wrestles with new biblical films and the hope of a better 'faith-based' cinema." *Los Angeles Times*, March 30, 2018. https://www.latimes.com/entertainment/movies/la-ca-mn-faith-based-movies-chang-20180330-htmlstory.html.

Cronk, Harold, dir. *God's Not Dead*. Greg Jenkins Productions, Pure Flix Entertainment, and Red Entertainment Group, 2014. 1 hr., 53 min.

Bibliography

Dawson, Roxann, dir. *Breakthrough*. Twentieth Century Fox, 2019. 1hr., 56 min.

Day, Heather. "Use of Stories in Courses and Student Engagement at Southwestern Michigan College." PhD diss. In Hall, Kenley D. "Jesus, God's Story and Storyteller," 12. Faculty Publications, Digital Commons @ Andrews University, 2019. https://digitalcommons.andrews.edu/pubs/1241.

Elliott, Belinda. "What's So Bad about The Shack?" Christian Broadcasting Network, June 15, 2022. https://www1.cbn.com/books/whats-so-bad-about-the-shack.

Erwin, Andrew, and Jon Erwin, dir. *I Can Only Imagine*. Erwin Brothers Entertainment, Kevin Downes Productions, and Mission Pictures International, 2018. 1hr., 50 min.

Faith and Leadership. "Traditioned Innovation." Duke University. https://faithandleadership.com/traditioned-innovation.

Foster, Richard J. *Celebration of Discipline Special Anniversary Edition: The Path to Spiritual Growth*. Rep. ed. New York HarperCollins, 2018.

———, et al. *A Spiritual Formation Workbook: Small-Group Resources for Nurturing Christian Growth*. New York: HarperCollins Publishers, 1999.

Fuster, Jeremy. "10 Highest Grossing Christian-Themed Movies, From 'The Ten Commandments' to 'God's Not Dead.'" *The Wrap*. https://www.thewrap.com/highest-grossing-christian-movies-ben-hur-passion-of-the-christ/.

Garber, Zev, ed. *Mel Gibson's Passion: The Film, the Controversy, and Its Implications*. Lafayette: Purdue University Press, 2006. https://doi.org/10.2307/j.ctt6wq6d1.

Gleiberman, Owen. "Film Review: 'The Shack.'" *Variety.*, March 2, 2017. https://variety.com/2017/film/reviews/the-shack-octavia-spencer-1202000189/.

Godawa, Brian. *Hollywood Worldviews: Watching Films with Wisdom & Discernment*. Downers Grove: Intervarsity, 2009.

Graybeal, Lynda L., and Julia L. Roller. *Learning from Jesus: A Spiritual Formation Guide (A Renovaré Resource)*. San Francisco: HarperOne, 2006.

Hale, Andy. "The Spiritual Discipline of Watching Film Together: A Conversation with Pop Theology's Ryan Parker." *CPF Podcast* (2020). https://cbfblog.com/2020/09/09/the-spiritual-discipline-of-watching-film-together-a-conversation-with-pop-theologys-ryan-parker/.

Hall, Kenley D. "Jesus, God's Story and Storyteller." Faculty Publications, Digital Commons @ Andrews University, 2019. https://digitalcommons.andrews.edu/pubs/1241.

Hamilton, Bethany., et al. *Soul Surfer: A True Story of Faith, Family, and Fighting to Get Back on the Board*. Illus. ed. New York: MTV, 2006.

Hauerwas, Stanley, and Willimon, William H. *Resident Aliens: Life in the Christian Colony*. Nashville: Abingdon, 1989.

Hazeldine, Stuart, dir. *The Shack*. Summit Entertainment, Gil Netter Productions, and Windblown Media, 2017. 2hrs., 12 min.

Higgins, Gareth. "Film Criticism as Spiritual Discipline, or What We Care About When We Care About Movies." Gareth Higgins: Storytelling, Spirituality, Cinema, Violence and Peace Blog, 2012. http://www.garethhiggins.net/blog-full/2012/03/26/film-criticism-as-spiritual-discipline.

———. *How Movies Helped Saved My Soul*. Lake Mary: Relevant Media Group, 2003.

Johnston, Robert. K. *Reel Spirituality: Theology and Film in Dialogue (Engaging Culture)*. Grand Rapids: Baker, 2000.

———., et al. *Deep Focus: Film and Theology in Dialogue,* Grand Rapids: Baker, 2019.

Jones, L. Gregory. *Christian Social Innovation: Renewing Wesleyan Witness*. Nashville: Abingdon, 2016.

Bibliography

"Josh Lucas Encourages Audiences Not to Dismiss "Breakthrough" As Just Another Faith-Based Film." BUILD Series, April 16, 2019. YouTube.com. https://youtu.be/3fhXen-5jfw.

Kendrick, Alex, dir. *Courageous*. Sherwood Pictures, Affirm Films, Tristar Pictures, and Provident Films, 2011. 2hrs., 9 min.

———, dir. *Facing the Giants*. Kendrick Brothers and Provident Films, 2006. 1hr., 51 min.

———, dir. *Flywheel*. Sherwood Pictures, 2003. 2hrs.

———, dir. *Overcomer*. Kendrick Brothers and Provident Films, 2019. 1hr., 59 min.

———, dir. *War Room*. TriStar Pictures, Affirm Films, Kendrick Brothers, and Provident Films, 2015. 2 hrs.

Kendrick Brothers. "Our Projects." https://kendrickbrothers.com/projects/.

Law, Jeannie Ortega. "Tim McGraw Speaks Out on 'The Shack' Controversy." *The Christian Post*, March 12, 2017. https://www.christianpost.com/news/tim-mcgraw-speaks-out-on-the-shack-controversy.html.

Lawrence, Brother Joseph de Beaufort. *The Practice of the Presence of God*. N.p.: Martino Fine, 2016.

Leading the Way. "Six Major Problems with The Shack." (February 24, 2017). https://www.ltw.org/read/articles/2017/03/six-major-problems-with-the-shack.

Leonard, Richard, SJ. *Movies that Matter: Reading Film though the Lens of Faith*. Chicago: Loyola University Press, 2006.

Mandisa. "Overcomer." (Deluxe Edition). iTunes. January 2013.

Mason, Anthony. "Powerful Salute: Hunger Games 'three fingered salute' now a widely-used protest symbol in South East Asia." CBS, May 12, 2021. YouTube. https://youtu.be/vNMYcIZjvNE.

McNamara, Sean, dir. *Soul Surfer*. TriStar Pictures, 2011. 1 hr., 52 min.

Merriam-Webster.com Dictionary. "Parable." https://www.merriam-webster.com/dictionary/parable.

———. "Story." https://www.merriam-webster.com/dictionary/story.

———. "Edutainment." https://www.merriam-webster.com/dictionary/edutainment.

———. "Koinonia." https://www.merriam-webster.com/dictionary/koinonia.

Merritt, James. *52 Weeks with Jesus: Fall in Love with the One Who Changed Everything*. Eugene: Harvest House, 2014.

"Movies with Strong Christian Content Are Flourishing—Movieguide | Movie Reviews for Christians." https://www.movieguide.org/news-articles/movies-strong-christian-content-flourishing.html.

National Geographic.org Resource Library. "Storytelling." https://education.nationalgeographic.org/resource/storytelling-x/.

Niemiec, Ryan M., and Danny Wedding. *Positive Psychology at the Movies: Using Films to Build Character Strengths and Well-Being 2*. 2nd ed. Toronto: Hogrefe, 2014.

Otto, Kevan, dir. *A Question of Faith*. Silver Lining Entertainment, 2017. 1 hr., 44 min.

Parker, J. Ryan. *Cinema as Pulpit: Sherwood Pictures and the Church Film Movement*. Jefferson: McFarland, 2012.

Phillips, Louise Gwenneth, and Tracey Bunda. *Research Through, With and As Storying*. New York: Routledge, 2018.

Pierce, Ashley, Adrian McDowall, and Craig Pickles, dirs. *Jesus: His Life*. Nutopia, 2019-. 43 min.

Bibliography

Plantinga, Carl. "The Power of Screen Stories." In *Screen Stories: Emotion and the Ethics of Engagement*. New York: Oxford University Press, 2018. https://doi.org/10.1093/oso/9780190867133.003.0002.

———. "The Rhetoric of Screen Stories." In *Screen Stories: Emotion and the Ethics of Engagement*. New York: Oxford University Press, 2018. https://doi.org/10.1093/oso/9780190867133.003.0003.

Renovaré. "Renovaré: Overview." https://renovare.org/about/overview.

———, "Renovaré: Spiritual Disciplines." https://renovare.org/about/ideas/spiritual-disciplines.

———, "Renovaré: Spiritual Formation." https://renovare.org/about/ideas/spiritual-formation.

Riggin, Patricia, dir. *Miracles from Heaven*. Columbia Pictures, Affirm Films, Roth Films, TDJ Enterprises, and Franklin Entertainment, 2016. 1hr., 49 min.

Rindge, Matthew S. *Bible and Film: The Basics*. New York: Routledge, 2021.

Salter McNeil, Brenda. *Roadmap to Reconciliation 2.0: Moving Communities into Unity, Wholeness and Justice*. Downers Grove: InterVarsity, 2020.

Simpson, Amy. "Mother to the Motherless: God showed me he is more than just my heavenly Father." *Today's Christian Woman* (May/June, 2012). https://www.todayschristianwoman.com/articles/2012/mayjune-issue/mother-to-motherless.html.

Sobczynski, Peter. "Reviews: The Shack." RogerEbert.com, March 3,2017. https://www.rogerebert.com/reviews/the-shack-2017.

Spencer, Christopher, dir. *Son of God*. Lightworkers Media, 2014. 2 hrs., 18 min.

Stoddart, Helen. "The Circus and Early Cinema: Gravity, Narrative, and Machines." *Studies in Popular Culture* 38, no. 1 (2015) 1–17. http://www.jstor.org/stable/44259582.

"T.C. Stallings Interview." *Faith On Film #112*, Apr 25, 2022. YouTube.com. https://youtu.be/YKOjfpCVbqc.

Wallace, Randall, dir. *Heaven Is for Real*. TriStar Pictures and Roth Films, 2014. 1hr., 39 min.

Walsh, John. *The Art of Storytelling: Easy Steps to Presenting an Unforgettable Story*. In Hall, Kenley D. "Jesus, God's Story and Storyteller," 13. Faculty Publications, Digital Commons @ Andrews University, 2019. https://digitalcommons.andrews.edu/pubs/1241.

Willard, Dallas. "Spiritual Formation: What It Is, and How It Is Done." https://dwillard.org/articles/spiritual-formation-what-it-is-and-how-it-is-done.

———. *The Spirit of the Disciplines: Understanding How God Changes Lives*. San Francisco: HarperOne, 2009.

Wilson, Jared. *The Storytelling God: Seeing the Glory of Jesus in His Parables*. Wheaton: Crossway, 2014.

www.ingramcontent.com/pod-product-compliance
Lightning Source LLC
Chambersburg PA
CBHW071213160426
43196CB00011B/2279